KEEP THE BAR
RAISED!

KEEP THE BAR RAISED!

STAYING SPIRITUALLY STRONG *after* YOUR MISSION

RALPH G. DEGN

CFI
Springville, Utah

© 2005 Ralph G. Degn

All Rights Reserved.

No part of this book may be reproduced in any form whatsoever, whether by graphic, visual, electronic, film, microfilm, tape recording, or any other means, without prior written permission of the author, except in the case of brief passages embodied in critical reviews and articles.

ISBN: 1-55517-732-8
e.1

Published by Cedar Fort Inc.
www.cedarfort.com

Distributed by:

Typeset by Natalie Roach
Cover design by Nicole Williams
Cover design © 2005 by Lyle Mortimer

Printed in the United States of America
10 9 8 7 6 5 4 3 2 1

Printed on acid-free paper

CONTENTS

Introduction—Stay Prepared for War	1
1. Raise Your Preparations for War	5
2. Weapons of War	15
3. Covenants	19
4. Commitments	25
5. Five Smooth Stones of Preparation	31
6. Enduring Well Your Trials of Faith	53
7. Become Again What You Once Were	67
8. Become What You Were Born to Be	71
9. The Stripling Solution	81
10. Raising Your Own Title of Liberty	89

INTRODUCTION
Stay Prepared for War

We live in troubled times—the beginning of even more troubled times.

—Boyd K. Packer

It was a hard-pitched battle. "Never had the Lamanites been known to fight with such exceedingly great strength and courage, no, not even from the beginning" (Alma 43:43). Against these difficult circumstances, Captain Moroni led the Nephites to victory.

As Moroni was negotiating surrender terms, the Lamanite leader, Zerahemnah, suddenly rushed forward with his sword to kill Moroni. But one of Moroni's soldiers struck the sword from Zerahemnah's hand. This alert soldier is only identified as "the soldier who stood by" (Alma 44:13). Though he may have been fatigued from the recent fierce fighting, and although peace negotiations were taking place, he was still vigilant and prepared for quick action.

This soldier "who stood by" was on standby, not merely a bystander. The dictionary defines one who is on standby as "one who can be relied on; ready or available for immediate action." One who is a bystander is defined as "one present but not participating; an onlooker, spectator." At the airport, the person who puts his name on the standby list is far more likely to get on the plane than is a bystander who merely wishes for a vacant seat.

During the October 2002 general conference, Elder M. Russell Ballard called not only for the bar to be raised for missionary preparation but also for missionaries to keep the bar raised upon their return home. (Read the next-to-last paragraph of his address.[1]) As a returned missionary, you too have fought valiantly. But like the soldier who stood by, you should still be prepared for sneak attacks, not letting down your guard.

As it was for Captain Moroni, so it is for the Lord—a soldier who stays prepared is invaluable. Because Mormon included this episode about the soldier who stood by, we understand the importance of remaining prepared after strenuous battles, even during an apparent cease-fire. Be like the soldier who stood by: Be on standby, not merely a bystander.

Recently the Lord's latter-day generals added some new counsel on preparation. To remain on standby in the later part of these latter days, days that President Packer has called "the beginning of even more troubled times,"[2] you must not only remain prepared for spiritual warfare, even during an apparent cease-fire, but you must also continually increase your preparation.

This new admonition from our leaders is the theme of this book.

Notes

1. M. Russell Ballard, "The Greatest Generation of Missionaries," *Ensign*, November 2002, 49.

2. Boyd K. Packer, "The Instrument of Your Mind and the Foundation of Your Character," Church Educational System satellite broadcast, 2 February 2002 (Salt Lake City: Intellectual Reserve, 2002), 2.

CHAPTER 1

Raise Your Preparations for War

The spiritual strength sufficient for our youth to stand firm just a few years ago will soon not be enough. Many of them are remarkable in their spiritual maturity and in their faith. But even the best of them are sorely tested. And the testing will become more severe.

—Henry B. Eyring

As a veteran of spiritual combat, you understand the importance of preparations for war. I'm sure that you, as a missionary, vowed to remain prepared upon your return home. Even so, I've found through surveys taken during several years of teaching a postmission preparation institute class that staying prepared for spiritual warfare once back in the lone and dreary world is a great challenge for all returned missionaries.

Because some returned missionaries are tired after serving so strenuously, they lose their proactive preparation for spiritual battle and shift into a sort of spiritual cruise control. But Satan isn't going to go easy on them just because of battle fatigue. Note the initiative the stripling warriors took when "they did assemble themselves together" (Alma 53:16) on their own. The record doesn't indicate that their parents or church leaders prodded them into this. In chapter 53, Alma lists an attribute that is directly responsible for their success. I believe Alma listed it to show the proactive nature of their righteousness: "They were exceedingly valiant for courage, and also for strength and activity" (Alma 53:20). Remember the verb the Prophet Joseph Smith used in writing the thirteenth article of faith? "We *seek* after these things"; we don't merely suggest them.

Other returned missionaries become "wearied and faint in [their] minds" (Hebrews 12:3), stop denying themselves (Matthew 16:24), and begin to slack off on the good habits they practiced in the mission field. As a result, they drift back to some premission habits that can cost them the companionship of the Spirit.

Even though you're now fighting on your home field, it doesn't mean the victory over Satan will be easier. Remember, you're still fighting an all-star opponent: Satan. He is "the father of all lies" (Moses 4:4), and he still seeks to deceive you and destroy your soul (D&C 50:3; 64:17).

Latter-day leaders have always stressed that we be prepared to fight the spiritual warfare that has been going on since our pre-earth life. President N. Eldon Tanner stated: "The war which was begun in heaven is raging here upon the earth; two great forces of right and wrong are pitted against each other. . . . We must have well-trained, disciplined, fearless, and loyal volunteers well equipped with the proper weapons of war and with a determination to win."[1]

President Harold B. Lee taught: "Preparedness is the way to victory. . . . Fear is the penalty of unpreparedness and aimless dawdling with opportunity. . . . Whether in physical or moral combat, the tide of victory rests with him who is prepared."[2]

Today our leaders are admonishing us to increase our preparation. Elder Henry B. Eyring said:

> Years ago, one of the things we taught people

we met as missionaries was that they could either progress or fall back spiritually. We told them it was dangerous to think they could stand still. I remember feeling it was true, and yet I wondered why it was so.

Time has taught me. As the forces around us increase in intensity, whatever spiritual strength was once sufficient will not be enough. And whatever growth in spiritual strength we once thought was possible, greater growth will be made available to us. Both the need for spiritual strength and the opportunity to acquire it will increase at rates which we underestimate at our peril.[3]

This is a new emphasis from our living prophets, who have the responsibility to see what kinds of new dangers we'll be facing and to tell us how to prepare our defenses in advance against them. They are like the ancient faithful watchmen on the towers who, instead of sitting or standing on their watch, walked and moved about on their rounds. Thus, they could see new dangers, no matter the source or direction (Ezekiel 3:17).

The Lord's latter-day generals' recent decision to put emphasis on increased preparation for spiritual warfare is exactly what Captain Moroni did. When Captain Moroni took command of the Nephite armies, he increased war preparations over what they had done in the past. First he "prepared his people with [armor]" (Alma 43:19). When the Lamanites also adopted armor, Captain Moroni then fortified the Nephite cities and lands (Alma 48:7–9). When the Lamanites developed strategies against these preparations, he fortified the cities even more, to the extent that the Lamanites were "exceedingly astonished" (Alma 49:9). Let's "liken [Captain Moroni's foresight] unto us, that it might be for our profit and learning" (1 Nephi 19:23).

Let's also see why his preparation astonished the Lamanites and how emulating his preparation can help us.

In abridging the Nephite records, Mormon took a lot of space to explain these increased defenses because he saw our day and knew what kind of warfare we would be fighting (Mormon 8:35). By way of comparison, let's use the Nephites to symbolize Church members in general and returned missionaries in particular, and let's use Lamanites and Amalickiahites to represent the evil spirits that follow Satan.

From Alma 49:1–3 we learn that the city of Ammonihah had been rebuilt. The Lamanites, who had destroyed the city less than ten years before, supposed that Ammonihah "would again become an easy prey for them" (Alma 49:3). Thus, they decided to attack an area they knew as a weak spot. But because the Nephites followed the instructions of Captain Moroni, they were no longer easy prey:

> [The Lamanites] fought with stones and with arrows. . . . But behold, how great was their disappointment; for behold, the Nephites had dug up a ridge of earth round about them, which was so high that the Lamanites could not cast their stones and their arrows at them that they might take effect. . . . Now at this time the chief captains of the Lamanites were astonished exceedingly, because of the wisdom of the Nephites in preparing their places of security. (Alma 49:2, 4–5)

Captain Moroni knew the enemy well, and he knew that they fought with stones and arrows. So he instructed the Nephites to build a defense that would stop stones and arrows. The Lord's leaders today also know the enemy well, and they are instructing us to raise the bar of our spiritual ridge of earth high enough so that Satan's latter-day spiritual stones and arrows won't take effect.

"Now the leaders of the Lamanites had supposed, because of the greatness of their numbers, . . . that they should easily overpower and subject their brethren to the yoke of bondage, or slay and massacre them according to their pleasure" (Alma 49:6–7).

President Wilford Woodruff taught, "Look at the number of devils we have, round about us! We have I should say, one hundred to every man, woman, and child."[4] If we are outnumbered one hundred to one by those with spiritual bondage and murder, and on their minds, you can see how much we need to heed our leaders' admonitions to raise the bar of our defenses!

> But behold, to [the Lamanites'] uttermost astonishment, [the Nephites] were prepared for them, in a manner which never had been known among the children of Lehi. Now they were prepared for the Lamanites, to battle after the manner of the instructions of Moroni.
>
> And it came to pass that the Lamanites, or the Amalickiahites, were exceedingly astonished at their manner of preparation for war. . . . For Moroni had altered the management of affairs among the Nephites, insomuch that the Lamanites were disappointed in their places of retreat and they could not come upon them.
>
> For they knew not that Moroni had fortified, or had built forts of security, for every city in all the land round about. . . . But behold, to their astonishment, the city of Noah, which had hitherto been a weak place, had now, by the means of Moroni, become strong. (Alma 49:8–9, 11, 13–14)

By following Captain Moroni's "instructions" or "manner of preparation" or "management of affairs," the Nephites turned their previously weak fortifications into strongholds. The Lamanites were "exceedingly astonished" and "disappointed" not only because they had never before encountered such strong defenses but also because they were done "in a manner which never had been known among the children of Lehi."

The Lord's latter-day generals have also given us "instructions," "manner[s] of preparation," and means to alter "the management of affairs" that will strengthen our spiritual defenses so that our weaknesses can become strong (Ether 12:27) "in a manner which [we] never [have] known" before.

Though the Nephites had tremendous successes with their increased preparations for defense in Alma chapter 49, chapter 50 begins by telling us, "Now it came to pass that Moroni did not stop making preparations for war" (v. 1). As you read the following verses, liken them to what our leaders today are asking us to do. Here's what Moroni did:

> He caused that his armies . . . should commence in digging heaps of earth round about all the cities throughout all the land. . . . And upon the tops of these ridges of earth he caused that there should be timbers, yea works of timbers built up to the height of a man, round about the cities.
>
> And he caused that upon those works of timbers there should be a frame of pickets built upon the timbers round about; and they were strong and high.
>
> And he caused towers to be erected that overlooked those works of pickets, and he caused places of security to be built upon those towers, that the stones and the arrows of the Lamanites

RAISE YOUR PREPARATIONS FOR WAR

could not hurt them.

And they were prepared that they could cast stones from the top thereof, according to their pleasure and their strength, and slay him who should attempt to approach the walls of the city.

Thus Moroni did prepare strongholds against the coming of their enemies, round about every city in all the land. (Alma 50:1–6)

Because of the increasing threats of invasion from the Lamanites, Captain Moroni continued raising the bar of his defensive preparations. He cast up heaps of earth around the cities, built works of timbers above the walls, constructed pickets above the works of timbers, and, finally, erected watchtowers above the pickets. This kind of preparation is what our latter-day watchmen are now emphasizing.

Here's what Elder M. Russell Ballard taught in his "raise the bar" general conference address:

> Today we are fighting a battle that in many ways is more perilous, more fraught with danger than the battle between the Nephites and the Lamanites. . . . We battle literally for the souls of men. The enemy is unforgiving and relentless. He is taking eternal prisoners at an alarming rate. And he shows no sign of letting up. While . . . many members of the Church . . . are doing great things in the battle for truth and right, I must honestly tell you it still is not enough.[5]

To be victorious in today's spiritual war, we need to be equipped with "the whole armour of God" (Ephesians 6:13). You've already utilized the whole armor of God in the mission field. But now the Lord's generals are warning you that during these "perilous times" (2 Timothy 3:1) in the last days, you need to be continually increasing your preparation in order to use that armor effectively.

To survive in the latter part of these latter days, you must be a spiritual special-operations soldier, one who is raising the bar in spiritual combat preparedness. Otherwise, your preparation may, as Elder Eyring warns, "soon not be enough."[6]

As a returned missionary, you have a head start on your preparation. Use your mission as a springboard for even better preparation. Your mission may have been the best two years of your life, but the coming years can be even better if you continually raise the bar in your "manner of preparation for war" (Alma 49:9).

President Gordon B. Hinckley has given us a great suggestion on how to keep raising the bar in our spiritual preparation. As you know, a suggestion from the prophet is really an admonition! The next chapter introduces President Hinckley's admonition.

Notes

1. N. Eldon Tanner, in Ardeth Greene Kapp, *What Latter-day Stripling Warriors Learn from Their Mothers* (Salt Lake City: Deseret Book, 1996), 16–17.

2. Harold B. Lee, *Stand Ye in Holy Places* (Salt Lake City: Deseret Book, 1974), 333.

3. Henry B. Eyring, "Always," *Ensign,* October 1999, 9.

4. Wilford Woodruff, in *Journal of Discourses,* 26 vols. (London: Latter-day Saints' Book Depot, 1854–86), 21:125–26.

5. M. Russell Ballard, "The Greatest Generation of Missionaries,"

Ensign, November 2002, 46–47.

6. Henry B. Eyring, "We Must Raise Our Sights," *Ensign,* September 2004, 14.

CHAPTER 2

Weapons of War

I recently received a proclamation from a group of LDS young men. . . . What a different world this would be if every young man could and would sign such a statement of promise. . . . It would be as if the stripling warriors of Helaman had recruited the youth of the world to their way of living.

—Gordon B. Hinckley

Anciently a soldier's most powerful weapon was his sword. He used it for both offense and defense. Today the most powerful spiritual weapon for both offense and defense is the "sword of the Spirit, which is the word of God" (Ephesians 6:17). One of the meanings of "word of God" is "covenant of God" (see next chapter). Therefore, when you keep your covenants, you're using your most powerful spiritual weapon. "Word of God" has other meanings—Jesus Christ, the scriptures, and the words of latter-day prophets.

The spiritual weapons included in Paul's "whole amour of God" can best be utilized by making commitments: commitments to yourself, to the Lord, and, even better, to yourself *and* the Lord. As a missionary, you worked every day to keep commitments. But once back home, you may begin to neglect making commitments. Remember that making and keeping commitments increases your chances for victory in today's spiritual battles.

During the October 1998 general conference priesthood session, President Gordon B. Hinckley admonished all young men to make and keep righteous commitments. "What a different world this would be if every young man could and would sign . . . a statement of promise," he said in reference to a pledge signed by a group of young men from nineteen stakes in northern California. He then asked that the young men in the Church "walk with a higher resolve, a determination to be Latter-day Saints in every meaning of the word."[1]

A "statement of promise," such as the one referred to by President Hinckley, would have the same effect as two powerful tools you used in the mission field: the *Missionary Handbook* and the commitment pattern.

The *Missionary Handbook* was written by the First Presidency and the Quorum of the Twelve Apostles as a summary of standards of conduct for missionaries. Our leaders thought it was necessary for missionaries to have, in addition to the standard works, a written summary of specific standards for the mission field that would help them to be the best missionaries possible. The commitment pattern is used by missionaries to help people make commitments to change and to live under the influence of the Spirit.

Whether you use these two powerful missionary tools or President Hinckley's suggestion of writing your own "statement of promise," the result is the same: You receive support from the Spirit in keeping your commitments to do the things you should, and you receive greater power to avoid doing the things you shouldn't.

President Hinckley has a marvelous, optimistic vision of

what the future holds for young people who increasingly prepare themselves for it: "May achievement, accomplishment, and service become your reward in the fascinating and wonderful life which lies ahead of you," he said."[2]

As you pledge to make and keep commitments, you raise the bar of your spiritual stoutness. Stout means brave, firm, sturdy, staunch, enduring, solid, and forceful. The latter part of these latter days is not a time for the spiritually out of shape or the faint of heart. Spiritually stout soldiers are the ones who spiritually stay in shape by making and keeping commitments.

The next chapter will discuss the most important commitments you can make—renewing and honoring the covenants you've made with the Lord.

Notes

1. Gordon B. Hinckley, "To the Boys and to the Men," *Ensign*, November 1998, 52.

2. Ibid.

CHAPTER 3

Covenants

There is a war going on, and we are engaged in it. It is the war between good and evil, and we are belligerents defending the good. We are therefore obliged to give preference to and protect all that is represented in the gospel of Jesus Christ, and we have made covenants to do it.

—Boyd K. Packer

The most powerful weapon in your arsenal of spiritual weapons of war is the sword of the Spirit, or the word of God (Ephesians 6:17). "In a broad sense, 'the word of God' means the teachings and commandments. At a more specific level, it is the sacred covenants between God and man."[1]

The making and keeping of covenants is based on the first law of heaven—obedience. Obedience to covenants is the keystone to excellence in everything in life and is an absolute necessity to victory in your spiritual, hand-to-hand combat with Satan.

The importance of covenants is one of the central messages of the Book of Mormon: "that they [the remnant of the house of Israel] may know the covenants of the Lord" (Book of Mormon title page). Early in the Book of Mormon, the Lord said to Nephi, "And inasmuch as ye shall keep my commandments, ye shall prosper in the land" (1 Nephi 2:20). This directive is repeated many times throughout the Book of Mormon to remind the Nephites—and us—of our responsibilities as residents of the promised land. Moroni concludes the Book of Mormon with a reference to "the covenant of the Father" (Moroni 10:33).

Obedience, or what Captain Moroni calls "maintenance of the sacred word of God," was what gave his army its victory over Zerahemnah (Alma 44:5). Disobedience by Amalickiah and Nephite dissenters, not the fact that the dissenters wanted another political system, is what concerned Captain Moroni (Alma 46). Obedience and faith are what gave the stripling warriors their strength, protection, deliverance, and victory, according to Helaman (Alma 57:21, 26). "Phrases such as 'keeping the commandments' (Alma 48:15), and 'maintenance of the sacred word of God' (Alma 44:5), [mean] living the covenants of the Lord (Alma 46:21)."[2]

Because "word of God" can mean "covenant of God," notice in Lehi's dream how important it is that we keep our covenants. "Whoso would hearken unto the word of God and would hold fast unto it, they would never perish; neither could the temptations and the fiery darts of the adversary overpower them unto blindness, to lead them away to destruction" (1 Nephi 15:24).

To not be overcome by the "mists of darkness [which] are the temptations of the devil which blindeth the eyes" (1 Nephi 12:17), we need to be "continually holding fast to the rod of iron," which is the word of God and the covenants of God (1 Nephi 8:30). Continually holding—not releasing one hand until the other hand has caught hold—is an adapt metaphor for continually renewing our covenants. Only by continually holding fast, not merely clinging, to our covenants is it possible for us to keep in our spiritual sight what we really want. Those who "continually [held] fast to the rod of iron . . . partook of the fruit of the tree" and stayed true (1 Nephi 8:30).

Of those who were only clinging to the rod after they partook of the fruit, Nephi says they became "ashamed" at the scoffing of others and "fell away into forbidden paths and were lost" (1 Nephi 8:25, 28). Clinging to the rod has about as much binding power as static electricity that causes clothes to cling. The force can be easily neutralized.

A returned missionary who remembers a few scriptures from his mission but fails to renew himself spiritually through daily scripture study is merely clinging to the rod. The same goes for those who hold a temple recommend but fail to renew their temple covenants through daily actions, weekly attendance at sacrament meeting, and frequent temple attendance. These clingers are easily distracted and spiritually blinded. We must do better. As Elder Boyd K. Packer has counseled, "We are . . . obliged to . . . protect all that is represented in the gospel of Jesus Christ"—including covenants.[3]

Here's an example of the importance of keeping your goals in sight:

> Florence Chadwick, the great long-distance swimmer, had already set the record for swimming the English Channel both ways. Now she wanted to be the first woman to swim from Catalina Island to the mainland, a distance of 26 miles. But this Fourth of July the ocean was an ice bath; the fog was so thick she couldn't see her support boat; sharks had to be driven away with rifle shots.
>
> Hour after hour she struggled through the frigid water. Her mother and trainer encouraged her from the boat, telling her it wasn't far, urging

her not to quit. But after 16 hours of seeing nothing but a thick fog bank ahead of her, she asked to be pulled into the boat. It wasn't until the boat landed a few minutes later that she realized there had been only a half mile to go. Still thawing out her chilled body a few hours later, she told reporters: "Look, I'm not making excuses, but if I could have seen land I could have made it."

It wasn't fatigue, cold water, or fear of sharks that defeated her, but fog: the fact that she couldn't see her goal. Two months later, on a clear day, she was the first woman to swim the channel, beating the men's record by two hours.[4]

Just as surely as Florence Chadwick was defeated by blinding fog, so you will be blinded and defeated by "mists of darkness" if you let go of the iron rod—your covenants with God. Covenant keeping makes it possible for you to keep in sight what is eternally important.

Notes

1. Lance Wickman, "Of Compasses and Covenants," *Ensign,* June 1996, 39.

2. Thomas A. Valletta, "The Captain and the Covenant," in *Alma, the Testimony of the Word,* ed. Monte S. Nyman and Charles D. Tate Jr. (Provo, Utah: BYU Religious Studies Center, 1991), 227.

3. Boyd K. Packer, *Memorable Stories and Parables of Boyd K. Packer* (Salt Lake City: Bookcraft, 1997), 23.

4. Joel Weldon, *Build a Better You* (Chicago: Nightingale-Conant Corporation, 1983), audiotape.

CHAPTER 4

Commitments

Commit thy way unto the Lord; trust in him; and he shall bring it to pass.

—Psalms 37:5

Stand fast in that liberty wherewith God has made [you] free.

—Alma 58:40

    Covenant keeping is absolutely essential to victory in spiritual warfare because it adds the power of the sword of the Spirit to your spiritual arsenal. And keeping righteous commitments strengthens the other parts of your armor.

    The consistent keeping of commitments, which includes your covenants, is a chief factor for spiritual and temporal success. Neglect of commitments, on the other hand, breeds failure. The reason commitments and covenants are so powerful in bringing victory in spiritual combat is that they allow you to add customized personal commandments to your life. Elder Hartman Rector Jr. said:

> I spent twenty-six years flying the navy's airplanes. It was very exciting to see how close I

could fly to the trees. This is called "flat hatting" in the navy, and it is extremely dangerous. When you are flying just high enough to miss the trees and your engine coughs once, you are in the trees.

Now let's pretend that the navy had a commandment—"Thou shalt not fly thy airplane in the trees." As a matter of fact, they did have such a commandment. In order to really be free of the commandment, it becomes necessary for me to add a commandment of my own to the navy's commandment, such as, "Thou shalt not fly thy airplane closer than five thousand feet to the trees." When you do this, you make the navy's commandment of not flying in the trees easy to live, and the safety factor is tremendously increased.

Admittedly, the latter commandment is your own addition, and care should be exercised that you do not get it mixed up with the law and expound it *as* the law. Rather, it is your own [personal] commandment, invented by you for your own self-preservation. . . . You should make up your own special and specific list of commandments. Such commandments would depend on your own past experiences and your own particular weaknesses.[1]

I believe that making your own list of personal commandments is a good example of what the Lord had in mind when he said:

> For behold, it is not meet that I should command in all things; for he that is compelled

> in all things, the same is a slothful servant; wherefore he receiveth no reward.
>
> Verily I say, men should be anxiously engaged in a good cause, and do many things of their own free will, and bring to pass much righteousness;
>
> For the power is in them, wherein they are agents unto themselves. And inasmuch as men do good they shall in nowise lose their reward.
>
> But he that doeth not anything until he is commanded, and receiveth a commandment with doubtful heart, and keepeth it with slothfulness, the same is damned. (D&C 58:26–29)

For returned missionaries, the model for using their agency for making personal commandments is the brave stripling warriors. Their prophet leader, Helaman, chronicled their steadfastness:

> But behold, they have received many wounds; nevertheless they stand fast in that liberty wherewith God has made them free [agency]; and they are strict to remember the Lord their God from day to day; yea, they do observe to keep his statutes, and his judgments, and his commandments continually; and their faith is strong in the prophecies concerning that which is to come. (Alma 58:40)

Lehi taught his sons that one of the reasons the Messiah would come was so that we could "act for [ourselves] and not to be acted upon" (2 Nephi 2:26). The Savior came to earth to preserve our agency, which we fought to protect during our pre-earth life (Moses 4:3). Lehi then gave this marvelous summation and warning:

> And now, my sons, I would that ye should look to the great Mediator, and hearken unto his great commandments; and be faithful unto his words, and choose eternal life, according to the will of his Holy Spirit;
> And not choose eternal death, according to the will of the flesh and the evil which is therein, which giveth the spirit of the devil power to captivate, to bring you down to hell, that he may reign over you in his own kingdom. (2 Nephi 2:28–29)

When we ignore the Holy Spirit, "we grant Satan power to captivate us through the corruptible elements within our bodies—just as the addict loses control to his physical addictions. Sin is an addictive substance. Our bodies become wired for it. That is what Father Lehi was teaching his sons."[2]

When we make daily, worthy commitments to act for ourselves, we are being "strict to remember the Lord [our] God from day to day" and to "observe to keep his statutes, and his judgments, and his commandments [including personal ones] continually." Don't be surprised, however, about the negativism you'll occasionally receive from some members of the Church regarding your efforts to maintain mission-field diligence.

For example, when I asked for input about this book from one Church member, he replied, "I'm not sure how many returned missionaries want to subject themselves to more rules and instructions, instead of letting down their hair a bit and getting on with life." Letting your hair down a bit is okay, but if you expect to "get on with life" successfully, you'll need to continue making commitments and honoring covenants.

Before we can keep commitments, or personal commandments, we must "prepare every needful thing" (D&C 109:8). Part of the whole armor of God is having your "feet shod with the preparation of the gospel of peace" (Ephesians 6:15). A soldier going into battle without wearing shoes is bound to stumble into trouble. Paul knew that when a soldier of his day fought against an enemy without foot protection, that soldier would be able to cut or stomp his enemy's feet and thus knock him off balance. It's easy to strike a mortal blow to an enemy who is off-balance. Having your spiritual feet shod with the "preparation of the gospel" brings peace because "if ye are prepared ye shall not fear" (D&C 38:30).

Each time you make a commitment and keep it, you allow the Spirit to tap into your reservoirs of creativity, willpower, skills, vision, and other attributes. You also allow the Spirit to actuate outside sources you need to accomplish your righteous desires. William H. Murray, organizer of the first successful ascent of Mt. Everest, made this insightful statement about commitment:

> Until one is committed, there is hesitancy, the chance to draw back, always ineffectiveness. There is one elemental truth, the ignorance of which kills countless ideas and splendid plans, that the moment one definitely commits oneself, then Providence moves too. All sorts of things begin to occur which would never otherwise have occurred, and a whole stream of events issues from the decision, raising in one's favor all manner of unforeseen incidents and material assistance which no man could have dreamt would have come his way.[3]

Much of your preparation for keeping commitments is

mental. You want to be like the stripling warriors, whose minds were firm and whose trust was in God (Alma 57:27). You must, as the Savior said, "prepare your minds" (3 Nephi 17:3) to receive or accomplish greater spiritual things. The next chapter describes five powerful methods to prepare your mind so you can remember and keep your commitments.

Notes

1. Hartman Rector Jr., "Live above the Law to Be Free," *Ensign,* January 1973, 131.

2. James L. Ferrell, *The Peacemaker* (Salt Lake City: Deseret Book, 2004), 156–57.

3. William H. Murray, in Mike McCaffrey, *Focus* (Chicago: Nightingale-Conant Corporation, 1983), audiotape.

CHAPTER 5

Five Smooth Stones of Preparation

And he . . . chose him five smooth stones out of the brook, and put them in a shepherd's bag which he had, . . . and his sling was in his hand: and he drew near to the Philistine.

—1 Samuel 17:40

David knew on whom he had to rely to come off victorious against Goliath, but he also knew that he had to prepare for battle: "I come to thee in the name of the Lord of hosts. . . . This day will the Lord deliver thee into mine hand . . . for the battle is the Lord's, and he will give you into our hands" (1 Samuel 17:45–47). So he took his shepherd's staff—a symbol of the Good Shepherd—in hand—a symbol of his working hand in hand with the Lord for the victory. Then he chose five smooth stones.

Alonzo L. Gaskill gives some interesting insights into the symbolism of the five stones.[1] The number five symbolizes two different ideas: God's grace and man in his fallen state. The number one symbolizes God, or being one with God. Thus, when David chose five stones, he was relying upon the grace of God to see him through defeating a man in his fallen state. The fact that David slew Goliath with only one stone symbolizes that he was one with God and that God intervened.

According to Gaskill, the number six symbolizes deficit, imperfection, evil, and opposition to and independence of God. "Curiously, Goliath was said to be six cubits and six inches tall (see 1 Samuel 17:4)." He wore six pieces of armor, and the head of his spear weighed six hundred shekels of iron (1 Samuel 17:7). He was the height of "opposition to and independence of God" and fit the proverbial "manifestation of evil."[2]

Because David prepared for combat by selecting five stones, I've divided mental preparation for spiritual combat into five steps, symbolizing that you also need God's grace to use these steps effectively to overcome a man in his fallen state—you. The more you use these stones, the more you'll be able to honor your commitments, provided you keep your staff in hand. Because these five steps require a high degree of focus, missionaries often neglect them when they return home. They are

- Decide
- Write
- Evaluate
- Bind
- Exercise the eye of faith

A returned missionary should be willing to do at least the first three steps as the minimum preparation for spiritual combat. Coach LaVell Edwards once said, "We can have the greatest will to do well, but unless we have prepared, our will to win is of little use. What is needed is the will to prepare! Those who have this will succeed."[3] The next step, bind, takes the greatest amount of courage and faith, and the final step, exercising an eye of faith, takes the most concentration. If you're not ready to do either of these last steps, wait until you are.

FIVE SMOOTH STONES OF PREPARATION

Decide

President Gordon B. Hinckley has suggested that young men, including returned missionaries, include in their "statement of promise" their recommitment to specific commandments.[4] The following material, therefore, is intended to help you keep personal commandments such as developing righteous desires, habits, attributes, and talents.

Decide comes from the Latin *decidere,* which means "to cut off" or "to cut the knot."[5] When you decide to do something, you literally cut off any retreat. When you decide not to do something, such as not to heed Satan's distractions and enticements, you cut off the "flaxen cord" with which Satan attempts to bind you (2 Nephi 26:22). To follow Church leaders' counsel to do more than you have in the past to prepare yourself for spiritual battle, you need to make a decision.

To be victorious in physical or spiritual warfare, you must decide to fight for your side and to avoid aiding the enemy. The philosopher Mencius said, "Men must be decided on what they will not do, and then they are able to act with vigor in what they ought to do."[6] If you won't do this, you'll be a "house divided against itself" (Matthew 12:25). Idling in indecision is not an attribute of a man or woman of God. Joshua said, "Choose you this day whom ye will serve" (Joshua 24:15). Elijah queried, "How long halt ye between two opinions?" (1 Kings 18:21).

To give your decisions extra momentum, base them on reasons. Reasons give you the *why* for your decisions—the fire for your deeds. Reasons help turn decisions into something you truly desire to do or become. Making decisions allows the Lord to grant unto you according to your desires (Alma 29:4). Desire is the prerequisite of faith, and decision, based on reasons, is the prerequisite of desire. If you want to accomplish a goal, develop or overcome of a habit, become a better person, or serve the Lord faithfully, you must first decide to do so. Then you will be capable of generating the desire necessary to accomplish your goal.

A key part in turning a choice into a decision is to sit down and carefully count its cost: "For which of you, intending to build a tower, sitteth not down first, and counteth the cost, whether he have sufficient to finish it? Lest haply, after he hath laid the foundation, and is not able to finish it, all that behold it begin to mock him" (Luke 14:28–29). Seek the Spirit before making decisions, and count the cost beforehand with these three questions:

- What am I willing to do to stick to my decision?
- What am I willing to give up to honor my decision?
- Am I really willing to make the necessary sacrifice to accomplish my decision?

Don't make important decisions when your judgment is impaired. During times of temptation, fatigue, inflamed emotions, peer pressure, or adversity, your judgment is compromised and your desires affected. Remember Florence Chadwick?

We don't usually make incorrect decisions intentionally. Rather, we simply fail beforehand to choose right. Aesop's fable of the grasshopper and the ant illustrates this. The grasshopper didn't deliberately decide to starve to death in the winter; he just didn't get around to deciding to store food in time. The ant, on the other hand, decided early in the summer to store food for the winter.

By making decisions in advance and with the right preparation, you save yourself the effort of having to make decisions under questionable circumstances. President Spencer W. Kimball said:

> You do not have to decide and redecide what you will do when you are confronted with the

same temptation time and time again. You need only to decide some things once. How great a blessing it is to be free of agonizing over and over again regarding a temptation. To do so is time-consuming and very risky . . . and each equivocation may result in error. There are some things Latter-day Saints do and other things we just don't do."[7]

One of the lessons of the parable of the ten virgins is deciding to prepare in advance for future events and not slipping into carelessness. Elder Bruce R. McConkie taught, "[The ten virgins are] not good and bad, not righteous and wicked, but *wise* and *foolish*. . . . All are members of the Church; the contrast is not between the wicked and the worthy. Instead, five are zealous and devoted, while five are inactive and lukewarm; ten have a testimony of Jesus, but only five are valiant therein."[8]

An alternate Greek translation uses "provident" rather than "wise": "They took care to make proper provision beforehand, and left nothing to be done at the last moment."[9] "Foolish" can also be translated as "careless," as in someone who "sees not what is proper and necessary."[10] To be provident is to be prepared, to decide beforehand what you're going to do in given situations.

I like to call personal commandments "provident promises," denoting a sense of being prepared, decided, dedicated, and careful. In particular, returned missionaries should make promises to themselves when it comes to dating, entertainment, work, and schooling. Here are some suggestions:

- Promise that the person you say good-bye to at the end of the date will be a little better than when you said hello.
- Promise that if lights get low and thoughts become even lower, you'll be like Joseph, who "got himself

out" (Genesis 39:12). As a bishop, I've heard some stories about pajama dances, hot tubs, and back rubs that ended sadly because someone didn't want to cause any embarrassment by leaving.

- Promise that you won't date anyone who isn't worthy right now to hold a temple recommend.
- Promise that you'll not watch R-rated (or worse) movies. Many returned missionaries have told me that they thought R-rated movies would not really be "that bad." But they observed that the Spirit withdrew from them while and after watching them. The same thing goes for many PG-13 movies and television programs.
- Promise to replace wrong thoughts with a hymn, as the First Presidency has suggested.[11]
- Promise to say no to fun when you really have to study or work.
- Promise that you'll save money—rather than go into debt—to buy items such as computers, TVs, bikes, entertainment centers, and so forth.
- Promise that you'll spend less time playing video and computer games and more time serving others.
- Promise that you'll always follow the prophet.
- Promise that you'll never let peer pressure make life's vital decisions for you.
- Promise to refrain from specific improper acts.
- Promise to accomplish significant goals and to develop good habits and attributes.

If you make a provident promise that you can't keep, admit it to yourself. Decrease your commitment to something you can accomplish. "And see that all these things are done in wisdom and order; for it is not requisite that a man should run faster than he has strength . . . [but] he should be diligent" (Mosiah 4:27).

WRITE

King Benjamin taught that if things of importance are not written, we are likely to value them less, become lax in following them, and even stray from what we originally believed. He taught that we must constantly remind ourselves of important things by having them "always before our eyes." We can't do this unless we write them down:

"I say unto you, my sons, were it not for . . . hav[ing] his commandments always before our eyes, that even our fathers would have dwindled in unbelief, and we should have been like unto . . . the Lamanites, who . . . do not believe them when they are taught them" (Mosiah 1:5).

The process of writing is as important as the product. Writing, even attempting to write your promise—not merely thinking about it—does three things:

- It clarifies your promise because you are forced to think about what is really involved in the promise.
- It causes you to evaluate whether you are really willing to pay the price to keep the promise.
- It gives you a sense of commitment because you feel your promise is more binding on you.

You are thus better prepared to come off conqueror in spiritual crises. If President Hinckley didn't think writing down commitments were important, he would not have asked us to sign our written pledge.

Every person will live life by either design or default. Life doesn't happen to you; it happens *from* you. In the mission field, missionaries who wrote down what they wanted to accomplish achieved much more than those who didn't. In a literal way, writing starts the physical creation of what, until being written, is merely a mental or spiritual creation.

One caution: Don't fall into analysis paralysis. Your promises are not meant to be written in stone like the Ten Commandments. You can frequently add to, subtract from, or change your promises as you think of better ways of expressing yourself. Don't avoid writing because you're having trouble coming up with just the right words. Anything written down is better than nothing!

Write your provident promises using what I call the "Five P's" to give you more purpose and power in keeping them:

Personal—Use the personal pronoun I: "I pay my tithing" instead of "Paying tithing is a commandment."

Present—Write them in the present tense, not future tense, to generate a "do it now" feeling: "I attend the temple" instead of "I will attend the temple."

Particular—Where appropriate, quantify: "I attend the temple weekly" instead of "I attend the temple frequently."

Positive—Write them as "I do" instead of "I don't do": "I attend only appropriate entertainment" instead of "I don't watch bad movies."

Possible—Leave out such adverbs as *always* and *only* until you truly can, with the Lord's help, always keep your commitment.

After writing your promises, review them frequently, keeping them "always before your eyes." Review them at least each Sunday. Other good opportunities to review them are when you're stuck in line or experiencing other delays.

C. S. Lewis, a favorite of Elder Neal A. Maxwell, understood the importance of reminding ourselves of our standards and commitment to live them. He said, "If you have once accepted Christianity, then some of its main doctrines shall *be deliberately held before your mind for some time every day*. . . . We have to

FIVE SMOOTH STONES OF PREPARATION

be *continually reminded* of what we believe. [No] belief... will automatically remain alive in the mind. It must be fed.... [If not,] *people simply drift away.*"[12]

Captain Moroni understood the importance of constantly reminding ourselves of our standards. That's why he caused "the title of liberty to be hoisted upon every tower which was in all the land" (Alma 46:36).

As you write and review your commitments, you hold "before your mind for some time every day" what you want to be "continually reminded of" so that you don't drift from what you want to do or become. You will not believe the power that this simple process of writing and reviewing gives you to avoid temptation! Here's a quote from a letter I received from one of our great missionaries just after he returned home:

> President, I want you to tell all of the returning missionaries just how eager Satan is to get us upon our return and for them to start on their Provident Promises list immediately upon getting home.
>
> I started on mine as soon as I got home. Here's the first one: "I am like Joseph in Egypt: I remove myself immediately from a situation that would influence me to lower my standards." This literally saved my life!
>
> I'd been home one week and received a call from [a former girlfriend], saying she was in town and she wanted to see me. I made sure my parents were going to be here and told her to come over. Everything went great. Two days later she gave me a call before flying back [home], telling me she had some questions about the Church and explained she was at a cousin's house.
>
> I cruised up to see her but no cousin. That's

when I started feeling uncomfortable. She told me her husband was in Japan, and I felt even more uncomfortable. Then she started sobbing, telling me how she still had feelings for me, threw her arms around me, and pushed up against me. At this point I think I was close to cardiac arrest. I quickly pushed her away and said I needed to go. While leaving, I told her that those feelings she had for me should be dead because she wasn't being fair to her husband.

I had difficulty driving home as I thought back at what could have happened. I never thought I'd be placed in a situation so scary! This was a big testimony booster for me of the power of my Provident Promises because the Spirit totally told me what to do. It was as if he had placed into my head the right words to say and into my body the courage to push her off and run like Joseph in Egypt, as I promised myself to do.

Tell the returning missionaries that if we don't have the Spirit with us, Satan's going to nail us. Provident Promises sure help![13]

Evaluate

I'm sure you recall reporting your missionary efforts to mission leaders and to the Lord. The Lord has always made "return and report" part of the stewardship of his servants. But when missionaries return home, many stop reporting and evaluating what they are doing, who they are becoming, and the direction they're going.

Make it a priority to evaluate and report your day to the Lord in evening prayer. I once heard President N. Eldon Tanner say that the majority of his evening prayer was spent in evaluating with the Lord what went right, what went wrong and why, and how he could have done better with his thoughts, words, and deeds that day.[14] Evaluating is also a great aid to staying focused and praying with real intent, especially when you're worn out at the end of the day.

Research shows that if you hear an idea and would like to adopt it into your life, there's only a 10 percent probability that you'll actually do it. If you decide to commit to yourself that you'll do it, your success rate increases to 25 percent. If you commit to someone else that you'll do it, the probability increases to 65 percent. However, if you not only commit to someone else but also set a specific time for reporting your efforts, the probability that you'll complete your commitment is 95 percent![15] Imagine the success you'll have when that someone you report to is the Lord!

The scriptures teach us to evaluate our efforts with such verbs as *observe, watch, and beware:*

- "And they did obey and observe to perform every word of command with exactness" (Alma 57:21).
- "Watch yourselves, and your thoughts, and your words, and your deeds, and observe the commandments of God" (Mosiah 4:30).
- "And I now give unto you a commandment to beware concerning yourselves, to give diligent heed to the words of eternal life" (D&C 84:43).

Also note in Abraham 4 the many references to preparing, organizing, and watching until what the Gods wanted to accomplish came to pass.

Evaluation is essential to winning teams as they review films of previous games. They see what worked, what didn't, why it didn't, and where improvements can be made. As a returned missionary, you'll fight your spiritual battles with much greater resolve and success if you evaluate by yourself and with the Lord how you are doing with your commitments.

BIND

The Lord said, "Bind yourselves to act in all holiness before me" (D&C 43:9). Among other definitions, *bind* means to protect, strengthen, firm up, bandage, commit, and "tie together by attachments of duty, gratitude, and affection."[16] Binding is an active, ongoing, frequently renewed process, not merely a one-time promise. We may bind ourselves before the Lord with either a covenant or a commitment, but there is a big difference between the two.

With a covenant, the Lord sets the terms. When we bind ourselves before the Lord through a covenant, we do it through an ordinance in a sacred setting. When we honor it, we literally become one with him, bound to him through the power of the priesthood. "I, the Lord, am bound when ye do what I say" (D&C 82:10). That is why binding through covenant is so powerful and why the word *covenant* should only be used in reference to sacred ordinances. It is why the Lord uses the word *bind* instead of another word.

When we bind ourselves before him in areas other than ordinances, we make commitments. We may set the terms of commitments but only for ourselves. We cannot set the terms for the Lord. We may petition the Lord for assistance, but we are in no way setting the terms by which he must abide. We are, however, promising to the Lord what we will do. We are binding ourselves before the Lord, not necessarily to or with him. Binding through a commitment is a way we may become partners with the Lord, if he so acquiesces. Elder Bruce R. McConkie taught this about binding oneself before the Lord with a commitment, or vow:

> As an incentive to greater personal righteousness, it is a wholesome and proper thing for the Saints to make frequent *vows* to the Lord. These are solemn promises to perform some duty, refrain from some sin, keep some commandment, or press forward in greater service in the kingdom. . . . Once [vows are] offered, they are to be kept (D&C 108:3; Numbers 30:2; Ecclesiastes 5:4–5). When vows are made in righteousness, they are sealed by the Holy Spirit of promise, and the Lord's blessings attend their performance. (D&C 132:7)[17]

The scriptures are full of admonitions for us to make commitments to the Lord. Here are two examples: "Nevertheless thy vows shall be offered up in righteousness on all days and at all times" (D&C 59:11). Vows can be considered as either covenants or commitments. "Commit thy works unto the Lord, and thy thoughts shall be established" (Proverbs 16:3). Look in the Topical Guide under "Oath," "Promise," "Commitment," and "Dedication" for more examples.

Missionaries who often bind themselves before the Lord through commitments in the mission field do so far less when they return home. However, the counsel we've received to commit doesn't apply strictly to missionaries. Speaking to members of the Church in October 2000, Elder H. Aldridge Gillespie taught, "Now is the time to 'bind [ourselves] to act in all holiness before [the Lord]' [D&C 43:9]. In other words, . . . we need to decide on specific actions to bring about needed changes in our lives."[18] And President Hinckley has expressed this hope: "I pray that not one [boy] will ever default on the promises he has made to himself, to the Church, and to the Lord."[19]

Notice that in 1 Nephi 3:15, where Nephi binds himself with an oath to retrieve the plates of brass, one of the footnotes to the verse refers to "Dedication" in the Topical Guide. Just as a temple is dedicated exclusively for the Lord's purposes, so you should be dedicated to keeping your commitments to the Lord. After all, you too are a temple of God (1 Corinthians 3:17).

Of the five steps of preparation I have listed for making and keeping commitments, binding yourself before the Lord takes the most courage and faith, but it is also the most powerful step because you make the Lord your partner in your quest. In addition, you are greatly motivated to go the extra mile.

To successfully bind yourself before the Lord, you need to understand two principles of faith in the Lord Jesus Christ. First, faith is not merely believing that the Lord can do something but rather that he *will* do something when it is his will. This brings us to the second principle, found in the Bible dictionary: "Prayer is the act by which the will of the Father and the will of the child are brought into correspondence with each other. The object of prayer is not to change the will of God, but to secure for ourselves and for others blessings that God is already willing to grant, but that are made conditional on our asking for them."

The best way to bind yourself before the Lord with a commitment is to actually make two promises in prayer: (1) "I promise I'll do _____ and ask thee to bless me with the power to do it." Along with this promise, if you have the faith, you'll also want to include some specific requests of the Lord to help you keep your promise. (2) "If I'm not successful in completing _____, I'll talk with thee about it immediately." If you don't make this second promise, you're setting yourself up for failure. That's because you'll feel too ashamed to approach the Lord since you'll feel you've failed him.

If your desire is to break a negative habit, promise something like this: (1) "I promise I will follow thy counsel in Proverbs 4:15: I'll 'avoid [my temptation and], pass not by it, [I'll] turn from it, and pass away.' I'll begin to 'turn from' _____ 'and pass away' and ask thee to bless me with the strength to complete my turn." (2) Make the same promise as in no. 2 above.

If you can't quite keep the terms of the promise you made with the Lord, apologize and lower the terms of your promise. Again, "it is not requisite that a man run faster than he has strength" (Mosiah 4:27). Commit to something that will stretch you less, but make it a commitment you can keep, with the Lord's help. As you become stronger, you can raise the terms. Your offering may be less, but the Lord will still accept it. In fact, he is eager to do so.

The important point is that you be honest with him and yourself about your ability to keep your promise. The Lord is desirous to help but on his timetable. Sometimes we must "wait upon the Lord" (Proverbs 20:22). If you are not ready to bind yourself before the Lord, then at least make a promise to yourself.

You practiced binding yourself before the Lord in the mission field and saw miraculous results. At home, if you are willing to exercise the courage and faith to bind yourself before the Lord, you will also see miraculous results because "Providence moves too. All sorts of things begin to occur which would never otherwise have occurred."[20]

Exercise the Eye of Faith

The fifth step to raising your ability to keep commitments is having an eye of faith. It is generally the least practiced of all the five steps because of the high degree of concentration and commitment it requires. But it can bring tremendous hope and encouragement as you imagine yourself relishing in the fruits of your success.

An eye of faith is what Alma says we should use to look

into the future and imagine ourselves receiving the fruits of our faith (Alma 32:40; 5:15). Mormon uses this expression to describe the process that many used to develop faith so strong that they finally saw with their physical eyes what they had only previously seen with their eye of faith (Ether 12:19). Paul said it this way, "Not having received [as yet] the promises, but having seen them afar off, and were persuaded of them, and embraced them" (Hebrews 11:13).

Today we call eye of faith our mind's eye or imagination, and we call seeing with an eye of faith visualization or mental rehearsal. Seeing with an eye of faith is a form of mental exertion that the Prophet Joseph Smith said we use when we exercise faith: "When a man works by faith he works by mental exertion. . . . It is by words . . . with which every man works when he works by faith."[21] If a picture is worth a thousand words, then the type of mental exertion that has the greatest effect on your ability to keep your commitments is forming a mental picture of yourself doing so.

As you imagine yourself with your eye of faith keeping your commitments, you are presenting evidence to your mind that what you have committed to do is possible. Elder Orson Pratt said, "Without evidence the mind cannot have faith in anything."[22] Going forward with faith depends to a great extent on how well you can imagine keeping your commitments.

Elder Pratt added, "The weakness or strength of faith will . . . be in proportion to the weakness or strength of the impressions produced upon the mind by evidence."[23] He warned that if your mind is "beclouded," no matter how strong the evidence you present to your mind, it will leave little impression and you will be left without faith.[24]

If you mentally practice keeping your commitments, you establish in your mind a habit for completing them. Mental rehearsal is one of the most powerful forms of the eye of faith because the "evidence" you present to your mind is so vivid, compelling, and impressionable.

Imagining yourself completing your commitments before you physically do so greatly facilitates your ability to complete them when you find yourself in the throes of spiritual warfare: "Victorious warriors win first and then go to war, while defeated warriors go to war first and then seek to win."[25] Stephen R. Covey has taught:

> When you visualize, you're exercising faith. Visualizing is a powerful mental process, one of man's unique endowments. Most of us neglect this power. Realize it or not, control it or not, the spiritual creation precedes the physical creation in all things. Most of life's battles are lost in this private phase. . . . I believe a person can resist and overcome temptation by creating a righteous response to temptation before it comes, by going through a mind making-up process involving four steps.
>
> First, feast on the words of Christ to cultivate a desire to know and do his will. Second, ask the Lord in sincere prayer to give you a heightened awareness of temptation and tempting environments whenever they arise. Third, promise the Lord that the moment he gives you such an awareness, you will immediately turn away and do something worthy—inwardly sing "I Need Thee Every Hour," review some memorized scriptures, or work on Church assignments. Fourth, see yourself in your mind's eye, confronting the temptation and replacing it with good. Complete the process by keeping the commitment.

KEEP THE BAR RAISED!

One young man who told me he had been tormented by unworthy thoughts for years tried this method and, after three months, testified that he had literally lost the disposition to think unclean thoughts.[26]

Whenever you exercise faith, you *will* face a trial of faith. This will take the form of difficulties, laziness, lack of desire, opposition from other people, or pressure to dishonor your commitments.

Practicing your eye of faith is vitally important because in times of pressure, when you're spiritually squeezed, what comes out is what's inside. For example, if water is poured into a plastic bottle and then squeezed for a drink, what comes out? Orange juice, root beer, lemonade? No. The same happens with you. What comes out of you when you're spiritually squeezed is what you've already put inside. Does a previously prepared and practiced decision flow forth, resulting in safety? Or does a lack of preparation and indecision ooze out, resulting in spiritual disaster?

Here's an example from the most famous ocean tragedy of all time, the *Titanic* disaster, which illustrates the vital necessity of preparation and practicing beforehand. In 1912 the *Titanic* was the largest and most luxurious ship ever built. But until 1911 the largest ship her captain had commanded was only about half her length and tonnage. Instead of giving the officers and crew several weeks of intensive shakedown cruises to acquaint them with the ship's handling capabilities, as was normal, the captain took only a few turns one afternoon. In addition, the crew didn't take time to decide upon and practice what to do in case of various emergency situations.

On the fateful night of April 14, 1912, when the first officer received warning from the crow's nest of "iceberg right ahead," he really didn't know what the *Titanic* could or could not do.

When the first officer was squeezed, lack of preparation came out because that's what was inside.

The board of inquiry investigating the tragedy found that the captain had "an indifference to danger" and that "overconfidence seems to have dulled his faculties usually so alert." As for the officers, the board found that they were "indifferent to danger, careless, perhaps simply too confident."[27] The *Titanic* disaster is a prime example of what happens when a lack of preparation and practice come face to face with an emergency. At the moment of decision, the time for preparation is past.

"Indifferent to danger, careless, perhaps simply too confident" is also a formula for spiritual disaster. Remember, "careless" was also used to describe the five foolish virgins. Here's Alonzo L. Gaskill's commentary on the ancient symbolism of the number five, which means both God's grace and man in his fallen state:

> The five wise [provident] virgins who have oil in their lamps, or testimonies, and righteousness in their hearts would be a representation of the grace of God. The five unwise [careless] virgins, of course, represent those who, in the spirit of fallen man as an "enemy" to God (Mosiah 3:19), have not prepared themselves for the coming of Christ.[28]

Will you take spiritual shakedown cruises with your eye of faith to mentally practice your commitments? If you do, you will be ready with a prepared and practiced response when trials of faith occur and spiritual icebergs threaten your course. President Tanner said, "Long before we are faced with [temptations], we . . . must have determined what our course will be. It is too late if we wait until the moment of temptation before making our decision."[29]

By using your eye of faith, you can assure that a disciplined, practiced decision flows from you when you are spiritually squeezed during spiritual hand-to-hand combat with Satan.

As you continually raise your level of preparedness by utilizing the five smooth stones of preparation, you make your provident promises easier to keep. Decide on your promises, write them down, evaluate them with the Lord, bind yourself before the Lord, and use your eye of faith to see yourself keeping your promises and enjoying their blessings.

Whenever you begin using these five stones of mental preparation for spiritual combat, you can be sure that you'll meet with trials of your faith. The next chapter warns you about what to look out for so that you can increase your faith and better endure the trials of your faith. As Elder Maxwell said, "The winds of tribulation, which blow out some men's candles of commitment, only fan the fires of faith of . . . special men."[30]

Notes

1. Alonzo L. Gaskill, *The Lost Language of Symbolism* (Salt Lake City: Deseret Book, 2003), 120–22.

2. Ibid., 121–22.

3. LaVell Edwards, *Achieving* (Salt Lake City: Randall Book, 1985), 67, 69–70.

4. Gordon B. Hinckley, "To the Boys and to the Men," *Ensign*, November 1998, 52.

5. *The Compact Edition of the Oxford English Dictionary*, 2 vols. (Oxford, England: Oxford University Press, 1971), 1:661.

6. Mencius, in *Bartlett's Familiar Quotations*, ed. Justin Kaplan (Boston:

Little, Brown and Co., 1992), 79.

7. Spencer W. Kimball, *President Kimball Speaks Out* (Salt Lake City: Deseret Book, 1981), 94.

8. Bruce R. McConkie, *Doctrinal New Testament Commentary*, 3 vols. (Salt Lake City: Bookcraft, 1965–73), 1:685.

9. Adam Clarke, *Clarke's Commentary* (Nashville: Abingdon, n.d.), 237.

10. Ibid.

11. *Hymns of The Church of Jesus Christ of Latter-day Saints* (Salt Lake City: The Church of Jesus Christ of Latter-day Saints, 1985), x.

12. C. S. Lewis, *Mere Christianity* (New York: Macmillan, 1952), 124; emphasis added.

13. Personal correspondence.

14. President Tanner expressed similar thoughts in *Prayer* (Salt Lake City: Deseret Book, 1977), 2.

15. Linda and Richard Eyre, *Teaching Children Responsibility* (Salt Lake City: Deseret Book, 1982), 135.

16. *Oxford Dictionary*, 1:217.

17. Bruce R. McConkie, *Mormon Doctrine*, 2d ed. (Salt Lake City: Bookcraft, 1966), 825.

18. H. Aldridge Gillespie, "The Blessing of Keeping the Sabbath Day Holy," *Ensign*, November 2000, 79.

19. Hinckley, "To the Boys and to the Men," 52.

20. William H. Murray, quoted in Mike McCaffrey, *Focus* (Chicago: Nightingale-Conant Corporation, 1983), audiotape.

21. Joseph Smith, *Lectures on Faith*, comp. N. B. Lundwall (Salt Lake City: Bookcraft, n.d.), 61.

22. Orson Pratt, "True Faith," in *Lectures on Faith*, 70.

23. Ibid., 71.

24. Ibid.

25. Sun-tsu, in *Bartlett's Familiar Quotations*, 80.

26. Stephen R. Covey, "Likening the Scriptures to Ourselves," *Ensign*, September 1974, 78.

27. Walter Lord, *The Night Lives On* (New York: William Morrow and Company, 1986), 204–5.

28. Alonzo L. Gaskill, *The Lost Language of Symbolism* (Salt Lake City: Deseret Book, 2003), 121.

29. N. Eldon Tanner, "Where Art Thou?" *Ensign*, December 1971, 34.

30. Neal A. Maxwell, "Why Not Now?" *Ensign*, November 1974, 12.

CHAPTER 6
Enduring Well Your Trials of Faith

My son, peace be unto thy soul; thine adversity and thine afflictions shall be but a small moment; and then, if thou endure it well, God shall exalt thee on high; thou shalt triumph over all thy foes.
—D&C 121:7–8

In your efforts to use the five smooth stones of preparation in spiritual warfare, trials of faith will come from three main sources: the Lord, you, and Satan. David's five smooth stones symbolize these trials of faith, no matter the source.

THE LORD

By choosing five stones, David symbolized that he was relying upon God's grace to see him through battle. But there is further symbolism in his use of the stones. David had faith in the Lord, and he knew that one stone would certainly be enough for the Lord and for a man of faith. But David also knew how the Lord works. Most of the time he proves and tries us before giving a blessing: "The Lord trieth the righteous" (Psalm 11:5). "For ye receive no witness until after the trial of your faith" (Ether 12:6).

In case the Lord wanted to try David's faith before guiding

the fatal shot, David would be prepared to allow for this with five stones, not just one. The message of the five stones is to be prepared to endure for a sustained period of time. Even though one stone is all the Lord needs, you need five to learn how to endure well the Lord's trying of your faith in him.

You

By far the greatest source of your trials of faith will come from your "natural man" (Mosiah 3:19)—when you're fatigued, when you lack patience, when you want quick-fix results. The natural man is tough to fight against.

Understand that you don't have to use all five stones all of the time to succeed at your promises. Just do the best you can. Whatever you do is better than doing nothing. Remember the caution given under the fifth "P" ("Possible") in writing your provident promises. Your promises are stars to guide you, not sticks to beat you.

The Lord understands that you are not yet perfect, and he doesn't condemn you as you attempt to grow with his help. He knows that growth is a process, requiring lots of practice: "And ye must practice virtue and holiness before me continually" (D&C 46:33). Spiritual gifts "are given for the benefit of those who love me and keep my commandments, and him that *seeketh* so to do" (D&C 46:9; emphasis added). Even the Lord himself had to develop gradually (D&C 93:12–14; Luke 2:52; Hebrews 5:8–9).

President Gordon B. Hinckley has taught: "I do not ask that you reach beyond your capacity. Please don't nag yourself with thoughts of failure. Do not set goals far beyond your capacity to achieve. Simply do what you can do, in the best way you know, and the Lord will accept of your effort."[1]

As much as you'd like to quickly see the results of your provident promises, things that are worthwhile take time to bring to pass. And at first, you may feel strange or uncomfortable using some of the stones of preparation, especially the stones of binding and having an eye of faith. You will particularly notice this when your promise is to replace a bad habit with a good one. You will have to overcome the tremendous discomfort of breaking an old habit while simultaneously cultivating a new one.

An interesting analogy from Dr. C. A. Riddle, somewhat modified here, teaches this.[2] It's based on an hourglass. At the bottom of the hourglass, you feel comfortable. You have lots of space to move around. You feel free. But as you begin to decrease the number of times you do your old, comfortable habit and start doing your new, difficult habit, you begin to feel restricted. It's as if you were moving upward toward the narrow neck of an hourglass. As you move upward, your comfort zone gets tighter. Soon you begin to notice how uncomfortable your new way of life is. You feel that your new habit threatens your freedom and is unnecessarily restrictive. As you move into the narrow neck, you feel more and more restricted. You may even feel like giving up. Some returned missionaries do give up, sinking back to pre-mission habits at the bottom of the hourglass.

But feelings of discomfort are temporary. They are the withdrawal symptoms of taking up your cross and denying yourself daily (Luke 9:23)—not monthly, quarterly, or yearly. If you tough it out, you will burst through the narrow neck of the hourglass and begin to feel less restricted by your new habit. "Wherefore gird up the loins of your mind, be sober, and hope to the end" (1 Peter 1:13).

As you continue to climb to the top half of the hourglass, you'll gradually feel more comfortable. Eventually you can become as God, the freest of all, having the real freedom of celestial living and not the restrictions of lesser kingdoms.

Benjamin Franklin used this analogy when he told of his struggles to develop new habits and break old ones:

> Like the man who in buying an ax of a smith, desired to have the whole of its surface as bright as the edge; the smith consented to grind it bright for him if he would turn the wheel. He turn'd while the smith press'd the broad face of the ax hard and heavy on the stone, which made the turning of it very fatiguing. The man came every now and then from the wheel to see how the work went on; and at length would take his ax as it was without further grinding. No, says the smith,
>
> Turn on, turn on; we shall have it bright by and by; as yet 'tis only speckled. Yes, says the man; but—I think I like a speckled ax best. And I believe this may have been the case with many who having . . . found the difficulty of obtaining good, & breaking bad habits, . . . have given up the struggle, & concluded that a speckled ax is best.[3]

Unless you replace the dirt you've just arduously dug out of a hole with concrete or some other fill, the same dirt will wash back into the hole with the first rain. I call this the "dirt-in-the-hole" principle. Captain Moroni didn't stop after he had "driven . . . out" the Lamanites. He then had the Nephites "go forth into" and "possess the land," replacing the Lamanites (Alma 50:9). Notice the forceful action verbs used to describe this replacement: "driven out," "go forth into," "possess."

David picked smooth stones because rough stones thrown from a sling are erratic in their flight; smooth stones, on the other hand, fly true and straight. Smooth stones have great symbolism. As you embark on your provident promises, you'll find that you may be inconsistent in staying true to them. But the more you practice and the more you use all five stones of preparation, the smoother will become your ability to keep your promises.

The first three steps (decide, write, evaluate), shouldn't give you much of a challenge, but the last two may. Don't give up; take a break if you have to.

For many years I've taught the practice of developing a written set of standards by which to live. As a bishop, mission president, and institute instructor, I learned that only about 50 percent of returned missionaries actually write down guiding standards. All 100 percent had good intentions of doing it and said they would do it, but half did not. Recall the parable of the ten virgins with regard to good intentions. Only half of them were provident.

Some returned missionaries say, "Why do I need to write down my standards? I already know what they are." James tells us, "But be ye doers of the word, and not hearers only, deceiving your own selves" (James 1:12). Remember Elder Henry B. Eyring's warning that no matter what you've been doing to "stand firm just a few years ago [it] will soon not be enough." If you haven't been writing down your promises, begin doing so. If you have written them down, evaluate them and then go the extra mile by doing the "Bind" and "Eye of Faith" steps.

Here's an example of the power of writing and reviewing. An Ivy League university conducted a study about the effect of written goals. Members of the graduating class of 1952 were asked whether they used written, daily goals. About 3 percent replied that they usually did; the remaining 97 percent said they used them rarely or not at all. The 3 percent had earned more than 80 percent of the A's earned by their class! In 1972 the survey was repeated. Researchers again found that about 3 percent used written goals. The net worth of that 3 percent was more than the combined net worth of the other 97 percent![4]

If writing is acknowledged as necessary for success in the world of business, will it be necessary for success in your postmission world? The Savior answered this question with the parable of the unjust steward (Luke 16:1–12). Elder James E. Talmage said, "Our Lord's purpose was to show the contrast between the care, thoughtfulness, and devotion of men engaged in the money-making affairs of earth, and the halfhearted ways of many who are professedly striving for eternal riches."[5] Elder Bruce R. McConkie said, "Ye saints of God, be as wise and prudent in spiritual things as the unjust steward was in worldly things."[6]

We must also overcome our "natural man" timidity and take more courage when it comes to fighting for righteousness. Elder Russell M. Nelson has taught, "We must realize that we are at war. The war began before the world was, and it will continue. The forces of the adversary are extant upon the earth. All our virtuous motives, if transmitted only by inertia and timidity, are no match for the resolute wickedness of those who oppose us."[7]

Satan

By now you understand that there will be times when you can't live up to your promises. Satan will try to convince you that you are too weak to keep your commitments and are thus a hypocrite for making and then breaking them. This is typical of Satan because he "seeketh that all men might be miserable like unto himself" (2 Nephi 2:27), and he "seeketh to destroy" (D&C 132:57). Some of the definitions in the Bible Dictionary for the devil are "slanderer," "adversary," and "spoiler."

Satan knows how extremely effective the five smooth stones of preparation are in combating him. That's why you will face tremendous opposition from him. You can be sure that he'll use discouragement and enticements to persuade you to quit. He'll use whatever it takes to keep you from honoring your provident promises.

Satan's tactics include the use of three "tions": temptations—"he inviteth and enticeth to sin" (Moroni 7:12); contentions—"Satan doth stir up the hearts of the people to contention" (D&C 10:63); and deceptions—he is the "father of all lies, to deceive and to blind men" (Moses 4:4).

He continually "maketh war with the saints" (D&C 76:29), and his most effective and frequent attacks are on your thoughts. The war in heaven is still being fought inside your head every second! In Orson Hyde's account of the First Vision, he makes this interesting observation: "The adversary benighted his [Joseph's] mind with doubts, and brought to his soul all kinds of improper pictures."[8] Doubts and improper pictures have always been some of Satan's most successful means of thwarting people from keeping the Spirit. Here's an example from another prophet:

When Heber J. Grant was first called as an apostle, he felt overwhelmed. For several months Elder Grant felt that he was unable to do the work of the Lord the way he felt the Savior wanted him to. Overpowering feelings of spiritual weakness and character imperfections plagued him. He later said:

> There are two spirits striving with us always, one telling us to continue our labor for good, and one telling us that with the faults and failings of our nature we are unworthy. I can truthfully say that from October 1882 until February 1883, that spirit followed me day and night, telling me that I was unworthy to be an apostle of the Church, and that I ought to resign. When I would testify of my knowledge that Jesus is the

Christ, the Son of the living God, the Redeemer of mankind, it seemed as though a voice would say to me: "You lie! You lie! You have never seen Him."[9]

Elder Grant had an experience in February 1883 when he was twenty-six years old that confirmed to him that he was called of God to be an apostle.[10] Most of your trials of enduring well will be related to thought control. Replace uninvited thoughts from Satan by taking the First Presidency's suggestion of humming a hymn. Controlling thoughts is like putting on "the helmet of salvation" to protect your head (Ephesians 6:17). Just as surely as you will perish in a physical war if you don't wear your helmet, you will perish in a spiritual war if you don't wear your helmet of thought control.

In the siege of Cuzco in 1536, 190 Spanish soldiers wearing steel helmets and vests defeated 200,000 Inca warriors armed with stones. Stones hurled from slingshots could kill or stun the soldiers, but the lone Spanish casualty in the siege was a soldier who failed to wear his helmet.[11]

Your head houses your command center. A chief objective in war is to knock out the enemy's command center, where all communications originate. Satan will try to disrupt your communications by whispering thoughts to you (2 Nephi 28:22). You can recognize them by their tone and the way they make you feel. If they are condescending and loud, or if they influence you to doubt or feel negative, they come from Satan.

Satan will attack you when you are making great spiritual strides or right after or before you receive an important calling. The Prophet Joseph Smith, Moses, and the Savior are examples. Satan will use the same tactics and sucker punches that you fell for before your mission, plus a lot of new ones. He especially knows he can get to you at "HALT" times—when you're hungry, angry, lonely, or tired. Stop him by saying, "Halt!"

As James taught, "Resist the devil, and he will flee from you" (James 4:7). Satan's efforts to overcome you during these dark times is well symbolized in Alma 55:29: "Many times did the Lamanites attempt to encircle them [the Nephites] about by night."

One of Satan's favorite ploys is described by James: "But every man is tempted, when he is drawn away of his own lust, and enticed" (James 1:14). James uses two descriptive and exacting expressions to show how Satan customizes our temptations to our weaknesses. The first expression is "drawn away" and refers to how hunters lure wild game out of the safety and protection of thick brush into an area set with snares. The second expression is "enticed." The word comes from fishing and means "to bait or catch with bait."[12] Satan uses the lusts of the flesh to lure us and entice us away from the protection that our covenants and provident promises give us.

Alma 47 shows another aspect of how Satan entices us. In this chapter, most of the Lamanite army didn't want to go to war against the Nephites. They appointed a leader named Lehonti, who fled with his men to a mountaintop. Amalickiah, a turncoat Nephite and the leader of the Lamanite army, sent a secret embassy by night to coax Lehonti down from the mount. Amalickiah wanted to speak with him, but Lehonti refused this invitation, as well as two more.

Not to be denied, Amalickiah "went up into the mount, nearly to Lehonti's camp" (Alma 47:12). He invited Lehonti down again, this time saying he could bring his guards with him. He probably added, "You'll be perfectly safe because you'll have your guards with you. Besides, I only want to talk to you." Lehonti was suckered in and came down. Amalickiah made him an offer he couldn't refuse: something for nothing. But after Lehonti did Amalickiah's bidding, Amalickiah had no further use for him. So he "caused that one of his servants should administer poison by degrees to Lehonti, that he died" (Alma 47:18).

Let's liken this scripture to returned missionaries. A mountain is a symbol for the temple and the safety we derive from our temple covenants. Amalickiah is a type for Satan, who will try the same ruse on you as Amalickiah did on Lehonti: "Just come down a little from your mount; you'll still be safe. After all, you are a returned missionary. You can handle it. Besides, you know other returned missionaries who engage in this behavior."

Satan will say whatever it takes to entice you little by little. He thus tries to "administer [spiritual] poison by degrees" until you're in spiritual trouble. Author John Bytheway calls this method Satan's "lie upon lie, decept upon decept strategy"[13] of leading his captives carefully down to hell (2 Nephi 28:21).

Finally, you must not allow Satan to divert your attention from Christ. Don't allow your provident promises, or anything else, to become your center. Your covenants with the Lord must be your center. Your promises are merely a tool to help you do your part of "having done all" (Ephesians 6:13) in your partnership with Christ.

In Ephesians 6:11, Paul says to "put on the whole armour of God." In verse 13, he adds, "Take [it] unto you," showing that the armor is provided by God, not by you. When you put on armor supplied by our Heavenly Father, you'll "be able to withstand in the evil day [the times of temptation], and having done all, to stand." In referring to standing, the Lord added through the Prophet Joseph Smith the following counsel: "He that is slothful shall not be counted worthy to stand" (D&C 107:100), and "I will give him grace and assurance wherewith he may stand" (D&C 106:8).

Now consider the symbolism of the stones being small. The stones used in ancient warfare fit into a sling and were about the size of a golf ball. When compared to the size of an enemy's body, especially Goliath's, the stones were quite small.

Your provident promises are an example of the "small and simple things [by which] great things are brought to pass" (Alma 37:6). When consistently kept over time, they bring to pass remarkable spiritual growth. But even if it seems that your growth is slow, you are progressing.

What is happening inside of you is similar to the way bamboo grows. Most plants grow rapidly in the tropics, but when a bamboo seed begins to grow, it can remain in the ground for up to five years before a sprout even appears! But then, watch out! It can grow up to three feet in twenty-four hours, reach heights of 120 feet, and be as strong as soft steel! What happens during those five years is that the seed sends out miles of roots to support its later rapid growth.

This will happen to you. You are preparing your mind and spirit and developing your own spiritual root system as a necessary foundation to support your future growth. "Wherefore, be not weary in well-doing, for ye are laying the foundation of a great work. And out of small things proceedeth that which is great" (D&C 64:33). You just need to "be patient until you shall accomplish it" (D&C 11:19). You've laid "the foundation of a great work" in the mission field—for the Lord, for yourself, and for the people you taught. Now build upon that foundation, and continue to fashion your own miraculous future with the help of your provident promises.

David's five smooth, small stones symbolize being prepared to endure trials well. You frequently practiced these steps of preparation in the mission field. Don't neglect them now. Even returned missionaries are tried by the Lord and are distracted, enticed, drawn away, and attacked by Satan.

Let's conclude this chapter by likening this scripture to ourselves:

> These [provident promises] should be attended to with great earnestness. Let no man count them as small things; for there is much which lieth in futurity, pertaining to [yourself] which depends upon these things. You know, brethren, that a very large ship is benefited very much by a very small helm in the time of a storm, by being kept workways with the wind and the waves. Therefore, . . . let us cheerfully do all things that lie in our power; and then may we stand still, with the utmost assurance, to see the salvation of God, and for his arm to be revealed. (D&C 123:14–17)

Enduring well your trials of faith is the key to whether you will heed certain influences. As the next chapter shows, we must heed those influences that help us become what we once were.

Notes

1. Gordon B. Hinckley, "Rise to the Stature of the Divine within You," *Ensign,* November 1989, 96.

2. Grant A. Worth, *Do Your Prayers Bounce off the Ceiling?* (Salt Lake City: Deseret Book, 1982), 45–48.

3. *Benjamin Franklin Autobiography* (Norwalk, Conn.: Easton Press, 1976), 115; capitalization standardized.

4. Brian Tracy, *The Psychology of Achievement* (Chicago: Nightingale-Conant Corporation, 1984), audiotape.

5. James E. Talmage, *Jesus the Christ* (Salt Lake City: Deseret Book, 1976), 463.

6. Bruce R. McConkie, *Doctrinal New Testament Commentary,* 3 vols. (Salt Lake City: Bookcraft, 1965–73), 1:515.

7. Russell M. Nelson, *The Power within Us* (Salt Lake City: Deseret Book, 1988), 99.

8. Orson Hyde, in Milton V. Bachman Jr., *Joseph Smith's First Vision: Confirming Evidences and Contemporary Accounts* (Salt Lake City: Bookcraft, 1980), 174.

9. Heber J. Grant, *Gospel Standards,* comp. G. Homer Durham (Salt Lake City: The Improvement Era, 1994), 194–95.

10. Ibid., 195–96.

11. *Cambridge Illustrated History of Warfare,* ed. Geoffrey Parker (Cambridge, Mass.: Cambridge Press, 1995), 136.

12. In *The Life and Teachings of Jesus and His Apostles,* 2d ed. rev. (Salt Lake City: The Church of Jesus Christ of Latter-day Saints, 1979), 408.

13. John Bytheway, *Righteous Warriors* (Salt Lake City: Deseret Book, 2004), 43.

CHAPTER 7

Become Again What You Once Were

Therefore we ought to give the more earnest heed to the things which we have heard, lest at any time we should let them slip.

—Hebrews 2:1

The Sabbath is an ideal time for you to evaluate your progress and renew your covenants and commitments. Doing so allows you to spiritually create your life each Sunday before you live it. This gives you tremendous capacity to heed the Spirit and do as Nephi taught regarding those in the great and spacious building: "We heeded them not . . . for as many as heeded them, had fallen away" (1 Nephi 8:33–34). What you heed, you become indeed.

The Savior, of course, is our perfect example. "He suffered temptations but gave no heed unto them" (D&C 20:22). Both the Savior and Satan became what they are because of what they heeded. Elder Dallin H. Oaks has reminded missionaries of their postmission responsibility to heed the right voices: "Returned missionaries, are you still seeking to be converted, or are you caught up in the ways of the world?"[1]

As you work in partnership with the Lord, you must allow him to be your senior companion. You must make him the center, the rock-hard foundation of your efforts: "And now, my sons, remember, remember that it is upon the rock of our Redeemer, who is Christ, the Son of God, that ye must build your foundation" (Helaman 5:12).

If you become too self-reliant, your armor will lose its toughness and temper, which you need to withstand Satan's unceasing attacks. One of the tests ancient armorers used to determine whether their weapons had been tempered sufficiently was to look for their reflection in them. If they could see themselves, the weapons were strong and ready for battle. In working with the Lord, you must strive to have "his image in your countenance" (Alma 5:14).

A great metaphor in *The Man in the Iron Mask,* by Alexander Dumas, shows the power of putting off the natural man and putting on the whole armor of God. In the novel the aged musketeers embark on the seemingly impossible mission of switching wicked King Louis with his worthy twin brother, Philippe, whom Louis has locked up in a hidden prison. But it has been decades since the retired musketeers have actively used their former, fine-tuned fighting techniques, and in the interim, they've acquired some harmful habits.

Because this new mission would require all of their old skills in order for them to succeed, Aramis says, "We will have to become again what we once were." They do away with the bad habits, practice intensely, and fine-tune their fighting skills. Before the battle, they take off their everyday clothes and don their old uniforms (after enlarging them a bit), symbolizing that they have, indeed, become again what they once were. Of course, they come off victorious.

By putting off the natural man and putting on the full armor of God, you become what you once were. You wore this same armor in the premortal war in heaven and, to a certain extent, in the mission field while you battled for the souls of

God's children. You must wear this same armor now that your full-time mission has ended.

There's a big difference between who you are and what you are. You are a child of God. Satan and his devils are also children of God. But knowing who they were did not make a difference to them when they chose not to heed Father's plan. They were called to heed the Lord but chose not to.

The musketeers knew who they were. But who they were was not the issue. The issue is what they had become and what had become of their fighting skills. If they didn't get their skills back, their lives would be in jeopardy. It is the same with us. If we don't become again what we once were, developing the spiritual fighting skills we had in the pre-earth life, our spiritual lives on earth will be in jeopardy.

"Many are called but few are chosen," the Lord warns (D&C 121:40). To be chosen here, as you were in the pre-earth life, you must become again what you once were (D&C 138:55–56; Alma 13:3–6). The Lord will help you become chosen and called again to his royal army. But to receive his help, you must heed his voice and the voice of his servants. You must put forth extra effort to honor your covenants and commitments—effort that the Lord's generals are calling for: "There has been a day of calling, but the time has come for a day of choosing; and let those be chosen that are worthy" (D&C 105:35). What you choose determines if you are chosen.

As you become again what you once were, you will be better able to practice the gospel principle discussed in the next chapter. That principle is that each of us in the pre-earth life was given a specific mission to perform in this life. In other words, as you become again what you once were, you will be better able to become what you were born to be and do.

Note

1. Dallin H. Oaks, "The Challenge to Become," *Ensign,* November 2000, 33.

CHAPTER 8

Become What You Were Born to Be

We were selected and fore-ordained for the mission before the world was, that we had our parts allotted to us in this mortal state of existence as our Savior had His assigned to Him.

—George Q. Cannon

You are one of a kind! The Lord utilized your unique attributes, talents, gifts, strengths, and, yes, weaknesses, to further his work when you served him on your mission. The Lord also customized your mission experiences to tutor you to further your work—what President George Q. Cannon called your individual "mission before the world was."[1] In fact, your unique full-time mission, with its tutoring challenges, definite purpose and duration, symbolizes your unique overall life's mission, with its challenges and definite purpose and duration. To honorably complete your life's mission is to become what you were born to be.

You honorably complete your life's mission the same way you honorably completed your recent proselyting mission as you worked hard, followed the rules (in the *Missionary Handbook*), and obeyed your mission president. See how the introduction and conclusion in the *Missionary Handbook*, with only minor changes, apply directly to your life's mission and your provident promises:

> This handbook of essential information will be an important tool on your [life's] mission. Use it daily as a ready reference. You will receive additional information from the [Lord] as he deems necessary.
>
> To prepare for the challenges of your mission, learn the patterns and suggestions in this handbook. Use these guidelines for your personal safety and well-being. Learn to love your Heavenly Father, your [future] companion, and the people you work with. You will be guided by the Spirit to bring joy and happiness to the people of the world. This can contribute to your happiness, make you stronger in your mortal life, and lead you to eternal salvation.[2]

Your life's mission is composed of several mini-missions, one from which you recently received a release—although you are never really released from doing missionary work. The following pages contain some quotations from Church leaders and others about your overall life's mission. As you read these quotes, you'll see how President Gordon B. Hinckley's admonition that you live by a "statement of promise" has direct application to determining your life's mission and becoming what you were born to be.

Elder H. Burke Peterson taught the following about your life's mission:

> Do you think for a moment that Heavenly Father would have sent one of His children to this earth by accident, without the possibility

of a significant work to perform? . . . You were preserved to come to the earth in this time for a special purpose. Not just a few of you, but all of you. There are things for each of you to do that no one else can do as well as you. If you do not prepare to do them, they will not be done. Your mission is unique and distinctive for you. Please don't make another have to take your place. He or she can't do it as well as you can. If you will let Him, I testify that our Father in Heaven . . . will inspire you to know your special purpose here.[3]

Blaine M. Yorgason expresses this concept beautifully in his poem "The Monument":

> God,
> Before He sent His children to earth
> Gave each of them
> A very carefully selected package
> Of problems.
>
> These,
> He promised, smiling,
> Are yours alone. No one
> Else may have the blessings
> These problems will bring you.
>
> And only you
> Have the special talents and abilities
> That will be needed
> To make these problems
> Your servants.

> Now go down to your birth
> And your forgetfulness. Know that
> I love you beyond measure.
> These problems that I give you
> Are a symbol of that love.
>
> The monument you make of your life
> With the help of your problems
> Will be a symbol of your
> Love for me,
> Your Father.[4]

The gospel principle of a specific life's mission is also known among other good people through the light of Christ. Viktor Frankl, author of *Man's Search for Meaning* and a survivor of the Nazi death camps, recognized the concept of a specific mission in life for each person when he wrote:

"Everyone has his own specific vocation or mission in life; everyone must carry a concrete assignment that demands fulfillment. Therein he cannot be replaced, nor can his life be repeated. Thus, everyone's task is as unique as is his specific opportunity to implement it." Frankl believed that our mission is not invented by us but rather is inwardly "detected."[5]

Because of the light of Christ, each of us can have an inner awareness of our own uniqueness and particular mission. The words "My life has a plan, my life has a purpose" in the Primary song "I Will Follow God's Plan" denotes the same idea.[6]

President Kimball taught that we agreed to our missions in the pre-earth life: "In the world before we came here, faithful women were given certain assignments while faithful men were foreordained to certain priesthood tasks. While we do not now remember the particulars, this does not alter the glorious reality of what we once agreed to."[7] Shakespeare was right on target

BECOME WHAT YOU WERE BORN TO BE

when he said, "To thine own self be true."[8] Being your true self is being true to what you were born to be.

Elder Orson Hyde taught the same concept: "Then, if it be true that we entered into a covenant with the powers celestial, before we left our former homes, . . . it is not impossible that we signed the articles thereof with our own hands,—which articles may be retained in the archives above, to be presented to us when we rise from the dead, and be judged out of our own mouths, according to that which is written in the books."[9]

President Ezra Taft Benson said this about the importance of fulfilling our "foreordained mission" in these latter days:

> For nearly six thousand years, God has held you in reserve to make your appearance in the final days before the Second Coming of the Lord. God has saved for the final inning some of his strongest children. There has never been more expected of the faithful in such a short period of time as there is of us. Each day we personally make many decisions that show where our support will go. What remains to be seen is where each of us personally, now and in the future, will stand in this fight—and how tall we will stand. Will we be true to our last days' foreordained mission?[10]

In the premortal existence, you received training to prepare you as a member of the Lord's latter-day special-operations forces (D&C 138:56). In fact, you were recommended to lead out in the Lord's crucial battles for righteousness in the last days. Sister Sheri Dew gave a great talk on this subject titled "You Were Born to Lead":

> God, our Father, and His Son, Jesus Christ,

with Their perfect foreknowledge, recommended
. . . you to fulfill your mortal probation during
the most decisive period in the history of the
world. . . . Your premortal spiritual valor
indicated that you would have the courage and
the determination to face the world at its worst;
to do combat with the evil one during his heyday,
and in spite of it all, to be fearless in building the
kingdom of God. You simply must understand
this because you were born to lead. By virtue of
who you are, the covenants you have made, and
the fact that you are here now, in the eleventh
hour, [shows] you were born to lead.

. . . He recommended you for now, when
the stakes are so high; the day when His
kingdom is being established, never again to
be taken from the earth. The simple fact is that
our Father did not recommend Eve or Moses or
Nephi or countless magnificent exemplars for
this dispensation. He recommended you.

. . . Do you really think that God would have
left the last days to chance by sending men and
women He couldn't count on? . . . You were sent
now because Father's most trustworthy children
would be needed in the final decisive battle for
righteousness. That is who you are, and that is
who you've always been. So will you live up to
our Father's recommendation? Will you do what
you were born to do?[11]

This gospel principle of having a foreordained mission and being true to it has been well portrayed in some popular films, including *The Lion King* and *The Lord of the Rings*. In *The Lion King*, Simba runs away and begins living a self-indulgent lifestyle after his father, King Mufasa, dies. Some time later Simba has a vision of Mufasa, who says: "My son, you have forgotten me." Simba replies, "No, no." Mufasa continues, "You have forgotten who you are and so have forgotten me. Look inside yourself, Simba. You are more than what you have become. You must take your place in the circle of life." Simba replies, "How can I go back? I'm not what I used to be." Mufasa concludes, "You are my son and the one true king. Remember who you are. Remember, remember." Simba did some soul searching, returned home, and became the king.

Before Simba could return and assume the throne, he had to understand three essential things: (1) He had to recognize who he was—the son of a king born to be a king. (2) He had to realize that he was more than he had become. (3) He had to understand that to become what he was born to be, he had to muster the spiritual strength necessary to overcome adversity.

You must realize these same three important points because you too are the son or daughter of the King, and you were born to one day be a king or queen. To prepare you for this, the King tutored you in the pre-earth life and has called you in this life to be his full-time ambassador: "Even before they [the noble and great ones] were born, they, with many others, received their first lessons in the world of spirits and were prepared to come forth in the due time of the Lord to labor in his vineyard for the salvation of the souls of men" (D&C 138:56). Thus far, you have received excellent preparation to become what you were born to be.

Elder John H. Groberg has taught:

> Reaffirm in your lives the importance of at least three things: first, our Father in Heaven does have a specific mission for all of us to fulfill and perform while we are here upon this earth; second, that we can, here and now in this life,

discover what that mission is; and third, that with His help we can fulfill that mission and know and have assurance—here and now in this life—that we are doing that which is pleasing to our Father in Heaven.[12]

Elder Groberg said that we "discover" our mission; Viktor Frankl wrote that we "detect" it. A great aid for discovering our mission is our patriarchal blessing—our own personal scripture. A great aid for making our mission a reality is a "statement of promise" referred to by President Hinckley. I hope this chapter has given you some insights into why President Hinckley supports the practice of governing our lives by a written statement of promise.

As you heed the promises you made to the Lord during your mission and as you come to understand what God expects of you as one of his noble and great ones reserved for the latter days, you will find yourself becoming what you once were and what you were born to be. By becoming that person, you will qualify for a spiritual blessing discussed in the next chapter.

Notes

1. George Q. Cannon, *Gospel Truth,* 2 vols. (Salt Lake City: Zion's Book Store, 1957), 1:22.

2. *Missionary Handbook* (Salt Lake City: The Church of Jesus Christ of Latter-day Saints, 1986), 1, 55.

3. H. Burke Peterson, "Your Life Has a Purpose," *New Era,* May 1979, 4–5.

4. Blaine M. Yorgason, *Charlie's Monument* (Salt Lake City: Bookcraft, 1976), vi.

5. Viktor E. Frankl, *Man's Search for Meaning* (New York: Simon & Schuster, 1963), 172, 157.

6. "I Will Follow God's Plan," *Children's Songbook* (Salt Lake City: The Church of Jesus Christ of Latter-day Saints, 1989), 164.

7. Spencer W. Kimball, *Teachings of Spencer W. Kimball* (Salt Lake City: Bookcraft, 1982), 316.

8. Shakespeare, *Hamlet* 1.3.

9. Orson Hyde, in *Journal of Discourses*, 26 vols. (London: Latter-day Saints' Book Depot, 1854–86), 7:314–15.

10. Ezra Taft Benson, "In His Footsteps," in *1979 BYU Speeches of the Year* (Provo: BYU Publications & Graphics, 1980), 46–47.

11. Sheri L. Dew, "You Were Born to Lead, You Were Born for Glory," in *Brigham Young University 2003–2004 Speeches* (Provo: BYU Publications & Graphics, 2004), 157–58.

12. John H. Groberg, "What Is Your Mission?" in *1979 BYU Speeches of the Year* (Provo: BYU Publications & Graphics, 1980), 92.

CHAPTER 9

The Stripling Solution

What a different world this would be if every young man could and would sign such a statement of promise. . . . It would be as if the stripling warriors of Helaman had recruited the youth of the world to their way of living.

—Gordon B. Hinckley

The thing returned missionaries say they miss most about the mission field is the almost constant feeling of the Spirit. This came from their ongoing preparation for spiritual battle and from their missionary mantle. But now, back home and without that mantle, how can they maintain the Spirit and continually increase their preparation for spiritual battle, as Elder Henry B. Eyring has suggested?[1]

The solution to this challenge is found in the admonition of President Gordon B. Hinckley that we be recruited to the stripling warriors' "way of living."[2] This way of living follows the same principles of spiritual power you learned and practiced on your mission. As you practice the stripling way of living, you qualify yourself for the same extraordinary spiritual support the stripling warriors enjoyed. Let's see what it is.

Mormon said, "I cannot write the hundredth part of the things of my people" (Words of Mormon 1:5). And he only included what the Lord commanded him to write (3 Nephi 26:12). I believe he included so much information on the hard-to-engrave-on metal plates about the stripling warriors because the Lord knew that the youth of today, including returned missionaries, would need an example to emulate in order to qualify for the same divine protection in fighting their personal spiritual battles. What a blessing it is to have the Book of Mormon, which gives us such vital battle tactics!

Mormon wanted to show that the reason the stripling warriors had such spectacular success against enemy aggression was not because of their physical weapons of war. Their success came mainly because of their spiritual weapons. These they had honed to a fine edge because of their way of living.

Helaman give a penetrating insight into what constitutes the power of these spiritual weapons when he said that the two thousand stripling warriors would be "a great support" to the Nephite army: "And now behold, as they never had hitherto been a disadvantage to the Nephites, they became now at this period of time also a great support; for they took their weapons of war, and they would that Helaman should be their leader" (Alma 53:19).

But how could two thousand "greenies," who had never fought, be of "a great support" to tens of thousands of battle-experienced veterans? The answer is found in Mormon's last phrase: "And they would that Helaman should be their leader." In other words, they chose to follow the prophet.

Mormon then describes the "young men" who were well versed in using spiritual weapons of war, especially the sword of the Spirit: "And they were all young men . . . who were true at all times in whatsoever thing they were entrusted. Yea, they were men of truth and soberness, for they had been taught to keep the commandments of God and to walk uprightly before him . . . and they did obey and observe to perform every word of command with exactness" (Alma 53:20–21; 57:21).

Notice that Helaman didn't merely say, "They obeyed every command." He said, "They did obey and observe to perform [they did what they were told] every word of command [every part of every command] with exactness" [taking no shortcuts and making no excuses]. If ever there were words that describe wielding the sword of the Spirit, it is these. Keeping covenants and commitments with exactness is a prerequisite to effectively wielding the sword of the Spirit. Missionaries constantly hear about obedience because it is the "first law of heaven"—and of missions.

The "great support" these stripling warriors brought was the spiritual help that came from their obedience to the Lord. They may have been novices to physical battle, but they were veterans in spiritual warfare because they had already practiced following "every word of command" from the prophet "with exactness."

This is the same "great support" I saw the new missionaries, fresh from the Missionary Training Center, bring with them when they entered the mission field. Our veteran missionaries loved it when new ambassadors of the Lord arrived. Veteran missionaries were especially delighted when they were called to train one of these new warriors. I considered the calling of trainer the most sacred and important calling in the mission. Most of our new warriors performed "every word of command with exactness" and, thus, could wield the sword of the Spirit with potent effect.

Our son Matthew described to me why in army basic training new recruits have pounded into them the importance of obeying with exactness in battle. They are constantly given little tasks to perform just to test their ability to perform with exactness. All training is to accustom their minds to obey every order to perfection. Most of the younger soldiers don't understand the importance of this at first.

During Matt's basic training, bed sheets were pulled up to exactly four inches from the head of the bed, not three or five. Time for arising was exactly 5:30 A.M., even though getting up earlier would give soldiers more time to get ready. Matt got chewed out by a lieutenant colonel when he found Matt shaving at 5:28 A.M. Shoes had to be aligned a certain way on top of the locker with the laces tied and tucked inside, even though to be put on they had to be taken out and untied. Matt observed:

> Obeying orders with exactness is the only way we stay alive in war. Soldiers need to obey quickly and with perfection. When they do, there is order and the unit runs the way it is supposed to. When someone does it their own way, we are then only as strong as our weakest link. Those soldiers who wouldn't obey were useless—even worse, dangerous. On the battlefield, where a sniper can nab you at any time, orders are not questioned. It will cost you your life, or the life of those around you.

Then Matt put his finger on why obeying with exactness is so important: "Together we have synergy, with the whole being greater than the sum of the parts." To soldiers fighting a physical war, synergy means fighting as if they had the help of more soldiers. To soldiers fighting a spiritual war, synergy means fighting *with* greater numbers—with soldiers from the other side of the veil. These soldiers are not ordinary soldiers. They are battle-hardened, experienced, dedicated warriors who literally wield the sword of the Spirit with power and purpose!

The prophet Elisha taught this to his young servant when

the servant warned him that they were surrounded by a great host of enemy soldiers. Elisha said, "Fear not: for they that be with us are more than they that be with them. . . . And the Lord opened the eyes of the young man; and he saw: and, behold, the mountain was full of horses and chariots of fire round about Elisha" (2 Kings 6:16–17). The servant of Elisha, with his spiritual eyes opened, was able to see the multitudes of angel soldiers surrounding them on the mountainside.

I'm sure that returned missionaries can testify to receiving help from the other side of the veil. But recipients of help from that realm are not limited to missionaries. Elder Jeffrey R. Holland taught this to the general membership of the Church:

> In the gospel of Jesus Christ you have help from both sides of the veil and you must never forget that. When disappointment and discouragement strike . . . you remember and never forget that if our eyes could be opened we would see horses and chariots of fire as far as the eye can see riding at reckless speed to come to our protection. They will always be there, these armies of heaven, in defense of Abraham's seed.[3]

President Hinckley has told us, "You cannot afford to do anything that would place a curtain between you and the ministering of angels in your behalf."[4] Elder Spencer J. Condie has added, "I pray that you wonderful young men will . . . be worthy to *receive* ministering angels."[5] And in a fireside for young adults, President Boyd K. Packer taught, "If you will keep your body in a worthy, receptive [condition], you will be prompted, even have angels attend you. Angels will attend you and will 'speak [to you] by the power of the Holy Ghost.'"[6]

Each one of us needs the "great support" that these angel

soldiers bring to our battles against Satan and his devils because without them we are sorely outnumbered. President Wilford Woodruff warned us about this: "Look at the number of devils we have, round about us! We have I should say, one hundred to every man, woman, and child."[7] President Woodruff also said, "A Priest holds the keys of the ministering of angels. Never in my life, as an Apostle, as a Seventy, or as an Elder, have I ever had more of the protection of the Lord than while holding the office of Priest. The Lord revealed to me by visions, by revelations, and by the Holy Spirit, many things that lay before me."[8]

Paul said that each of us is a "temple of God" (1 Corinthians 3:16). And President John Taylor said the Lord sent Nephite spirits to protect the Logan Temple.[9] As you wield the sword of the Spirit, you too will receive "great support" from the army of the Lord's angel soldiers to protect your physical temple. We have been promised:

- "Be not afraid nor dismayed by reason of this great multitude; for the battle is not yours, but God's" (2 Chronicles 20:15).
- "The angel of the Lord encampeth round about them that fear him, and delivereth them" (Psalm 34:7).
- "For I will go before your face. I will be on your right hand and on your left, and my Spirit shall be in your hearts, and mine angels round about you, to bear you up" (D&C 84:88).

Satan has singled out for extra attention the leaders of the Lord's army, especially when they are young. Elder LeGrand Richards taught, "When [Satan and his followers] were cast out, that third of the host of heaven brought with them the knowledge that they had in the spirit world . . . and [they] knew whom [they] had fought against in that war in heaven." Elder Richards went on to teach that Satan wanted to destroy Moses and the Savior when they were babes and Joseph Smith when he was a young man. He knew that if he couldn't do so while they were young, he would later have to reckon with Moses and Joseph Smith as prophets and with the Savior as the Messiah.[10]

So it is with you. Satan is on an all-out campaign to defeat you here and now. He knows that this is an opportune time because you're trying to make difficult adjustments. And he knows that if he doesn't distract you now from qualifying for the Lord's protection of his angel soldiers, he will have to deal with you later when you are more powerful as a father, mother, and experienced leader in the Church.

The examples in the Book of Mormon are types and patterns for our day. Though we heard in the mission field that we were like the stripling warriors, I believe that the model of the stripling warriors fits returned missionaries better than it does missionaries in the field. This is because the stripling warriors fought battles in the world at large, not as the Lord's emissaries in the mission field.

Thus, the solution to the loss of the missionary mantle is the stripling solution. It is what you do to become again what you once were and to become what you were born to be. The stripling solution provides the added help of angel soldiers to surround you and be "a great support" in your spiritual battles against the hosts of Satan. You qualify yourself for the stripling solution just as the stripling warriors did—by practicing the stripling way of life as you follow the prophet "with exactness" and remain true to your covenants and commitments.

The next chapter will help you follow the prophet with exactness as you raise your own title of liberty.

Notes

1. Henry B. Eyring, "Always," *Ensign,* October 1999, 9.

2. Gordon B. Hinckley, "To the Boys and to the Men," *Ensign,* November 1998, 52.

3. Jeffrey R. Holland, "For Times of Trouble," *New Era,* October 1980, 15.

4. Gordon B. Hinckley, "Personal Worthiness to Exercise the Priesthood," *Ensign,* May 2002, 52–53.

5. Spencer J. Condie, "Becoming a Great Benefit to Our Fellow Beings," *Ensign,* May 2002, 45.

6. Boyd K. Packer, "The Instrument of Your Mind and the Foundation of Your Character," Church Educational System satellite broadcast, 2 February 2002 (Salt Lake City: Intellectual Reserve, 2002), 4.

7. Wilford Woodruff, in *Journal of Discourses,* 26 vols. (London: Latter-day Saints' Book Depot, 1854–86), 21:125–26.

8. Wilford Woodruff, in Condie, "Being a Great Benefit to Our Fellow Beings," 46.

9. John Taylor, in Nolan P. Olsen, *Logan Temple: The First 100 Years* (Logan, Utah: Watkins Printing, 1978), 172.

10. LeGrand Richards, "Call of the Prophets" *Ensign,* May 1981, 32.

CHAPTER 10

Raising Your Own Title of Liberty

Behold, whosoever will maintain this title [of liberty] upon the land, let them come forth in the strength of the Lord, and enter into a covenant that they will maintain their rights and their religion, that the Lord God may bless them.

—Alma 46:20

You raise your own title of liberty as you fulfill President Gordon B. Hinckley's admonition of writing your own "statement of promise"—your provident promises. This is the spiritual equivalent to what the Nephites did physically when they "came running together with their armor girded . . . [and] rending their garments in token, or as a covenant that they would not . . . be ashamed to take upon them the name of Christ" (Alma 46:21).

Why did Captain Moroni call his torn coat a "title" of liberty, instead of a banner, flag, or ensign? The answer is that the word *title* means "an established right to something; anything that provides a basis for a claim."[1] The torn coat that Captain Moroni waved was a symbol of the real title. He had written on it the blessings the Nephites could claim because of their obedience to the real title of liberty: the covenants they had entered into with the Lord. Their covenant keeping established their right and basis for a claim to be free from bondage in the war they were fighting against Nephite dissenters who had broken their covenants.

Just as the ancient title of liberty listed what the Nephites were fighting for and symbolized their covenants, so your provident promises—your own title of liberty, if you will—show what you are committed to fight for and symbolize the covenants you have made. As with the Nephites, so it is with us. The real title to our liberty is honoring our covenants with the Lord Jesus Christ, the source of our liberty.

Your covenant keeping makes possible your wielding the most powerful weapon in spiritual battles: "the sword of the Spirit, which is the word of God" (Ephesians 6:17). Your provident promises will help you "put on" the other parts of the "whole armor of God" that Paul mentions in Ephesians 6:14–16. Honoring your covenants and commitments gives you the freedom to be your best self—a "leading [person] who [has] influence . . . [one who is] in high places who could persuade many others not to become servants to Satan."[2]

Here's a suggestion from Elder Robert D. Hales that has helped many returned missionaries write down their commitments: Choose a slogan that describes the cause for which you are fighting.[3] Having a cause to fight for has always been vital to warriors. When David's jealous older brother, Eliab, tried to persuade David to return home from the battlefield, David refused, saying, "Is there not a cause?" (1 Samuel 17:29). The word *cause* appears numerous times in the index of the triple combination to the "war chapters" in the Book of Mormon (Alma 43–63). Here are some examples.

Captain Moroni's armies, though vastly outnumbered, were "inspired by a better cause, for they . . . were fighting for . . . their liberties" (Alma 43:45). The stripling warriors had a cause: "to fight in all cases to protect the Nephites and themselves from bondage . . . and were fixed with a determination to conquer our enemies, and to maintain . . . the cause of our liberty" (Alma 53:17; 58:12).

Fighting for "the cause of our liberty" is an extremely important theme in the Book of Mormon. In fact, Mormon gave more space to this topic than to the Savior's personal ministry. Because he was writing for our day, you understand the importance of fighting for our liberty. You have this same cause too—the cause you fought for in the pre-earth life. It is the freedom to return to our eternal home, the freedom from the chains and captivity of Satan.

To inspire yourself, choose a slogan that sums up your cause and helps you, as Paul says, "fight the good fight of faith" (1 Timothy 6:12). In a seminar for mission presidents, Elder Hales suggested that "Return with Honor" is a good slogan for anyone.[4] "Keep Your Armor Bright," from Brigham Young, is another good slogan.[5] In the movie *Rudy*, Notre Dame football players leaving the locker room for the field pass a door, above which is a sign that reads, "Play Like a Champion Today."

I have placed my slogan—*Realize Milagres!* ("Work Miracles!"), from Mosiah 8:18—above the light switch by the door of my home office. Write your slogan on a sign and fix it to your mirror or on a wall by the door. Touch it whenever you leave as a reminder of what you are about that day.

The Lord teaches us through our senses, including the sense of touch. In fact, the English word *token* comes from the Latin verb *tango*, meaning "to touch."[6] Many returned missionaries who speak a Romance language will recognize this. The Spanish and Portuguese form is *tocar*. A token, or touch, is a powerful form of impressing a concept upon the mind.

You raise your own title of liberty as you write down your provident promises and as you believe and embrace a cause.

You become as the stripling warriors, more prepared to handle the lures and distractions of Satan and the adversity and disappointments of the world.

In conclusion, here are three challenges that apply to returned missionaries. The first is from Elder Dallin H. Oaks:

> What does it mean to be true to the faith? That word *true* implies *commitment, integrity, endurance,* and *courage*. It reminds us of the Book of Mormon's description of the 2,000 young warriors: . . . "they were men who were true at all times in whatsoever thing they were entrusted. Yea, they were men of truth and soberness, for they had been taught to keep the commandments of God and to walk uprightly before him" (Alma 53:20–21).
>
> In the spirit of that description I say to our returned missionaries—men and women who have made covenants to serve the Lord and who have already served Him in the great work of proclaiming the gospel and perfecting the Saints—are you being true to the faith? Do you have the faith and continuing commitment to demonstrate the principles of the gospel in your own lives, consistently? You have served well, but do you, like the pioneers, have the courage and the consistency to be true to the faith and to endure to the end?[7]

This following challenge is from President Hinckley given to a group of missionaries in the field:

> I want to challenge you to keep the faith. Don't say, "That chapter in my life is behind

me." Stay on your mission for the rest of your days. Have the spirit with you the rest of your days. Continue to study, to read the scriptures. Continue to work, to serve the Lord. Continue to keep the commandments and live as you ought to live. Be good fathers, good mothers, good husbands, good wives, good people in the community. Get all the education you can get and get it with study and faith.

Hold true to the Iron Rod throughout your days. Nearly every missionary does but, unfortunately, there's one here and another there who drifts away.

I want to give you a challenge to be faithful to this cause and kingdom of God our Eternal Father and the risen Lord Jesus Christ as long as you live, and fill every responsibility that you are asked to fill.

I don't hesitate to promise you in the name of the Lord that if you do so your lives will be fruitful and happy, and the Lord will open the windows of heaven and pour down blessings upon you.[8]

Here again is President Hinckley's challenge and promise, given this time with "returned missionaries" or "returned missionary" substituted in the appropriate places:

> You are not wasting your lives in drifting aimlessly. Returned missionaries have purpose. Returned missionaries have design. Returned missionaries have plans that can only lead to growth and strength.
>
> When your energies are harnessed, when

your dreams are focused, marvelous things happen. I recently received a proclamation from a group of returned missionaries. . . .

I compliment every returned missionary who signed this pledge. I pray that not one will ever default on the promises he has made to himself, to the Church, and to the Lord.

What a different world this would be if every returned missionary could and would sign such a statement of promise. . . . It would be as if the stripling warriors of Helaman had recruited the returned missionaries of the world to their way of living. . . .

God bless you returned missionaries . . . of this, His great Church. May each of you walk with a higher resolve, a determination to be a Latter-day Saint in every meaning of the word. May achievement, accomplishment, and service become your reward in the fascinating and wonderful life which lies ahead of you.[9]

Walking with "higher resolve" calls for preparation with higher resolve. This is the kind of resolve that comes by following President Hinckley's admonishment to pledge to live by and sign a "statement of promise." This is the kind of resolve you expected from your investigators when you, using the commitment pattern, asked them, "Will you . . . ?"

Now, will you raise your own title of liberty? Will you raise it so you can heed Elder Eyring's warning? Here it is again: "The spiritual strength sufficient for our youth to stand firm just a few years ago will soon not be enough . . . and the testing will become more severe."[10]

As a returned missionary, you are familiar with testing. As a full-time missionary, you went through spiritual boot camp in the MTC. Then, out in the field, you experienced full combat training and front-line battle conditions. Finally, you agonized through spiritual hand-to-hand combat. But now, even this training and experience "will soon not be enough." To spiritually survive in the latter part of the latter days, you'll need even more training.

The Lord's generals have been pointing us toward this advanced preparation. Every six months at general conference, Church leaders give us timely instruction to strengthen and prepare us. And our prophet, President Gordon B. Hinckley, has written two books, showing us the *Way to Be!* and the importance of *Standing for Something*.

At an organization meeting for the Institute Men's Association, Elder Eyring told us, "The most underused resource in the Church is that of the returned missionaries." Choose not to be an underused resource. In the past you chose to qualify yourself to be part of the Lord's latter-day army when you served as a full-time missionary. Don't let your training and preparation go to waste. Stay ready for spiritual combat, and increase your postmission preparation for the difficult days that lie ahead.

Research published in *BYU Studies* found that "the most important thing [returned missionaries] can do to help themselves during this [postmission] stage is to continue to maintain the good spiritual habits" of their mission. The article also stated that there is a "strong correlation . . . between early post-mission private religiosity and later adult private religiosity."[11] In other words, if returned missionaries are serious about their post-mission preparation, they are likely to keep the spiritual bar raised as they get older.

As an experienced spiritual warrior, you'll appreciate these concluding words of one of history's great warriors. In his last major address as prime minister, and while war was still raging in the Pacific, Winston Churchill said this to his countrymen: "I told you hard things at the beginning of [this war]; you did not shrink, and I should be unworthy of your confidence . . . if I did not still cry; Forward, unflinching, unswerving, indomitable, till the whole task is done and the whole world is safe and clean."[12]

You were told some hard things at the beginning of this book. But as you work to remain prepared and to continually increase your preparation for spiritual warfare, you will move forward with faith—"unflinching, unswerving, indomitable."

Will you raise your own title of liberty and seek protection from the stripling solution in order to compensate for the loss of your missionary mantle?

Will you heed what you once heeded so that you can become again what you once were? Will you do it now so that you can become what you were born to be?

Will you continually increase your preparation for spiritual combat so that you can be a soldier who stands by, one whom the Lord can rely on at a moment's notice?

Will "you walk with a higher resolve, a determination to be a Latter-day Saint in every meaning of the word [so that] achievement, accomplishment, and service become your reward in the fascinating and wonderful life which lies ahead of you"?

I know you can. And I know you want to. May the Lord bless you in your righteous desires to keep the bar raised so that you can do your part in preparing the world for the Master's second coming.

Notes

1. *The Compact Edition of the Oxford English Dictionary,* 2 vols. (Oxford, England: Oxford University Press, 1971), 2:3335.

2. Spencer W. Kimball, *The Miracle of Forgiveness* (Salt Lake City: Bookcraft, 1969), 175.

3. Robert D. Hales, "The Aaronic Priesthood: Return with Honor," *Ensign*, May 1990, 39.

4. Ibid. Elder Hales repeated this statement in his May 1990 conference address.

5. Brigham Young Journal History, LDS Historical Department Library, 5 October 1856, 1.

6. *Burt's Latin-English Dictionary* (New York: A. L. Burt Company, n.d.), 195.

7. Dallin H. Oaks, "Following the Pioneers," *Ensign*, November 1997, 73.

8. Gordon B. Hinckley, "Returned Missionaries," *Church News*, 1 March 1997, 2.

9. Gordon B. Hinckley, "To the Boys and to the Men," *Ensign*, November 1998, 51–52.

10. Henry B. Eyring, "We Must Raise Our Sights," *Ensign*, November 2004, 14.

11. Robert J. McClendon and Bruce A. Chadwick, "Latter-day Saint Returned Missionaries in the United States: A Survey on Religious Activity and Postmission Adjustment," *BYU Studies* 43, no. 2 (2004): 152, 148.

12. In Sheri L. Dew, *No One Can Take Your Place* (Salt Lake City: Deseret Book, 2004), 80.

ABOUT THE AUTHOR

Ralph G. Degn earned his bachelor's degree in history from the University of Utah and his master's degree in Latin American studies from Georgetown University. He is the founder of Fireworks West Internationale, which has provided fireworks for such events as the 2005 Presidential Inauguration, 2002 Winter Olympics, and several Super Bowls.

A former mayor, Brother Degn has been the piano player at the Pickleville Playhouse for more than twenty-five years. He has served as an organist, institute teacher, Boy Scout leader, and bishop. In addition, he served as mission president of the Brazil São Paulo North Mission from 1993 to 1996 and as a founding adviser for the Institute Men's Association.

Brother Degn is the author of *Keep the Spirit* and *Title of Liberty*. He and his wife, Mary Ann, live in Wellsville, Utah. They are the parents of eight children.

If you would like a copy of Brother Degn's *Title of Liberty* booklet, written to help missionaries keep track of their "provident promises" and spiritual progress, send a self-addressed, stamped envelope (two first-class stamps) and $1 to the author at 251 E. 100 North, Wellsville, Utah, 84339.